GOAL!

Intimate portraits and interviews with
every living FIFA World Cup™ Final scorer

Michael Donald

hamlyn

If you have ever dreamt of scoring a goal in the World Cup Final, this book is dedicated to you.

An Hachette UK Company
www.hachette.co.uk

First published in Great Britain in 2017 by
Hamlyn, a division of
Octopus Publishing Group Ltd
Carmelite House
50 Victoria Embankment
London EC4Y 0DZ
www.octopusbooks.co.uk
www.octopusbooksusa.com

Manufactured under license by Octopus Publishing Group

Distributed in the US by
Hachette Book Group
1290 Avenue of the Americas
4th and 5th Floors
New York, NY 10104

Distributed in Canada by
Canadian Manda Group
664 Annette Street
Toronto, Ontario, Canada M6S 2C8

ISBN 978-0-60063-508-6

A CIP catalogue record for this book is available
from the British Library.

Printed and bound in China.

10 9 8 7 6 5 4 3 2 1

Publishing Director Trevor Davies
Senior Editor Pauline Bache
Copyeditor Robert Anderson
Creative Director Jonathan Christie
Designer Jeremy Tilston at The Oak Studio
Picture Research Manager Giulia Hetherington
Senior Production Manager Katherine Hockley

CONTENTS

PREFACE

This book features portraits of, and interviews with, all the FIFA World Cup™ Final goalscorers who were alive at the time of the 2014 FIFA World Cup™. Every one of them took part in the project. Those players who are no longer with us may not actually feature here but it is intended that they are very much here in spirit. Every player to have ever scored a goal in a FIFA World Cup™ Final is credited in the Statistics section on pages 204-21.

I stood on the empty pitch at the Estadio Centenario in Montevideo (below), in Uruguay, where the first ever FIFA World Cup™ Final was held in 1930, with the ball from that match in my hands. The hairs stood up on the back of my neck. While those players from the past cannot be included because they are no longer with us, this book is intended to be a tribute to them, just as much as it is to those who are included in these pages.

INTRODUCTION

I can't remember exactly what I was researching at the time that I came up with the idea for this book, but it did not take long to work out just how few people had ever scored a goal in a FIFA World Cup™ Final. At the time it was 54, of whom 34 were alive. I thought it would be a great idea to photograph and interview them all. That was 12 years ago.

When I was pitching the idea, I would say, "Imagine you are on your travels and you find yourself in some far-flung land with a friend. You are in a little bar and your friend says to you, 'See that old man over there?' There is an old man sitting in the corner quietly minding his own business. 'He scored a goal in the World Cup Final.' In slight disbelief, you politely approach the old man. He did score a goal in the World Cup Final, and he spends the next half an hour telling you all about it. You come away knowing you will never see that goal in quite the same light again. That is the motivation behind this book."

Since its inception in 1930, only 58 people have ever scored a goal in the FIFA World Cup™ Final (excluding the penalty shoot-outs of 1994 and 2006). When I began this project, 34 of them were alive. That number included bathroom salesman Dick Nanninga, vintner Paolo Rossi and retired insurance salesman Martin Peters. It did not include Johan Cruyff, Diego Maradona, David Beckham or Lionel Messi. It remains the most exclusive club in football. This is not some debatable pantheon – you are either in or out.

The project took a team of us to Brazil, Argentina, Uruguay, Turkey, the Czech Republic, France, Germany, Spain, Italy, Belgium and England over a period of six years. Many of the older players did not live the fabulous lifestyles we now associate with top-level footballers. The first player we shot was Dutch player Dick Nanninga. Very self-effacing about his achievement, he was a bathroom salesman at the time, in Belgium, and loved his job. During the interview in his home he asked his wife to find his runners-up medal from 1978. She came back with the box it had come in but inside was a medal he had won for singing karaoke. She did eventually find the right one. He took us to his local bar afterwards where most of the regulars knew him. The barmaid asked me what we were all doing there. I explained that we where here because of Dick. She asked, "What's Dick done?" In all the years he had been going there, he had failed to mention that he had scored a goal in the 1978 FIFA World Cup™ Final.

When we shot Carlos Alberto Torres at the Maracaña Stadium in Rio I wanted to shoot him in the players' tunnel that runs underground from the changing rooms to the pitch. The stadium was open to the public, so for convenience they only agreed to close the tunnel for as short a time as possible, so there would not be a big build-up of people at either end. As we were setting up, members of the public were walking through the tunnel to the pitch and back. I had my assistant, Stevie, stand in so I could light the picture before we got Carlos Alberto in. People were walking through looking at Stevie wondering who he was, thinking he must be famous. When Carlos Alberto came down, understanding what I was doing he stood behind Stevie waiting until we were ready. The people walking through kept looking at Stevie, wondering who he was and assuming that the quiet guy standing just behind him was the security, which only added to the interest in Stevie. When they swapped places, it quickly dawned on the passing fans that the "security" was in fact the scorer of the greatest goal in World Cup Final history. In the ensuing chaos, we did need the real security.

This disparate group of individuals share two things. They all scored goals in a FIFA World Cup™ Final, and they all felt both privileged and humbled by the experience. For me, it was a humbling experience to meet them all and spend time with them, take their photographs and hear their stories. I got to hold the 1930 FIFA World Cup™ Final ball in my hands in Montevideo. I did headers with Pelé in São Paolo. I took penalties in the Olympiastadion in Munich with Paul Breitner. I nearly went home with Emmanuel Petit's winner's medal in my pocket in Paris. I shared a beer with Josef Masopust at Dukla Praha and I was asked to leave the Mangiunhos favela in Rio at gunpoint.

This project was completed in 2014 when the FIFA World Cup™ returned to Brazil. At that time all 34 goalscorers who appear in this book were alive. At the time of writing, of those 34, Alcides Ghiggia, Josef Masopust, Zito, Carlos Alberto Torres and Dick Nanninga have sadly passed away.

In great sporting moments, we are all spectators, commentators, pundits and fans. These men were not spectators. They did not just witness the moment; they were the moment. There are now only 29 people on the planet who can honestly say, "I scored a goal in a World Cup Final." This is their story.

© FIFA TM

Alcides

GHIGGIA

TEAM	**Uruguay**
BORN	**22 December 1926–16 July 2015**
THE MATCH	**In 1950 the FIFA World Cup™ was hosted by Brazil. The final was played on 16 July in the Estádio de Maracanã, Rio de Janeiro.**
ATTENDANCE	**199,954**
RESULT	**Brazil 1-2 Uruguay**
THE GOAL	**In the 79th minute Ghiggia scored the winning goal.**
PHOTOGRAPHED	**at Bar Montevideo Sur, in Montevideo Old Town**

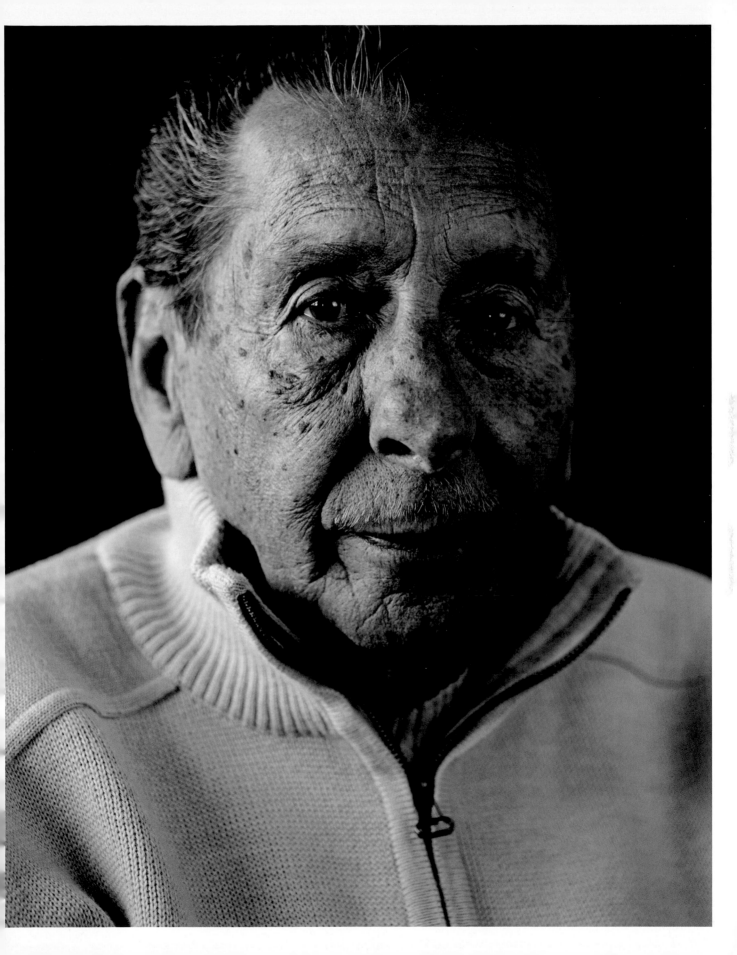

After a 12-year break, because of the Second World War, the FIFA World Cup™ resumed in 1950. The competition was played, for the first and last time, using a league system rather than the current knockout system, in the latter stages. As it turned out, the only teams that could win, Brazil and Uruguay, met for the last game, making it, for all intents and purposes, the final. A draw, however, would see the Brazilians take the trophy.

Some 200,000 Brazil fans packed into the newly built Maracanã Stadium in Rio, to watch what they believed would be a certain victory over Uruguay. Brazil had come off a 6-1 demolition of Spain and an even more convincing 7-1 victory over Sweden. Uruguay had only drawn with Spain and scraped past Sweden with an 84-minute winner. Most of the Uruguayan delegation left the night before the final so sure were they of defeat.

"I was only 22 years old. Before the final I wasn't nervous at all. The older players were. I think they felt more weight on their shoulders.

"Usually one team would come out and then the other. Our captain was smart enough to take us out to the field at the same time as the Brazilians, because we knew that, if the Brazilians went out first, they would clap and cheer and, if we came out after, they would whistle. We went out together so it felt like they were clapping us."

As everyone expected, Brazil dominated the first half, but the Uruguayans managed to hold their own, even managing two close attempts on goal.

"It was 0-0 at half-time. They came out and scored after two minutes. The linesman put his flag up for offside and then put it down again. Obdulio [Varela], our captain, grabbed the ball and went to complain to the linesman and the referee came too. It was on the other side of the pitch from me so I couldn't hear them, but I knew Obdulio didn't speak any English and George Reader, the English referee, didn't speak any Spanish. That lasted some time, but they gave the goal.

Friaça had shot low past the keeper to become the first Brazilian to score in a FIFA World Cup™ Final and sent the masses in the stands into ecstasy. However, at 66 minutes Ghiggia beat his man on the right and sent in a low cross that was converted by Juan Alberto Schiaffino high into the corner of the net.

"The Brazilians seemed to freeze. The crowd wasn't cheering. I realised we could win it.

"It was the 79th minute. I was very quick, very fast. I escaped Bigode, and on my left Juvenal could not reach me so I lined myself up diagonally across the goal. I think [Moacir] Barbosa [the Brazilian keeper] thought I was going to centre the ball so he came out a little bit so as to cut out my centre kick, and he left me a space. I was coming in on the run and

↓ **Schiaffino scores the equaliser for Uruguay in the 66th minute.**

I put the ball right beside the post and when he dived the ball was already in the net.

"There was silence.

"We kept on playing till the end, when Brazil had a corner. The ball came through the air. I couldn't see the referee. I was looking at the ball and saw Gambetta going to grab the ball with his hands. I thought, 'This guy is crazy, it's going to be a penalty,' but I looked away and saw the referee whistling for the end of the game.

"We were happy. We hugged each other. We even did a lap of honour, but it was ... I don't know, it was something. There were 30 or 40 Uruguayans and the rest were all Brazilians. But, despite the joy we had, it was sad to see the stands – you could see people desperate and crying, you know? There was a little bit of sadness inside me. It was impressive – the sadness that overcame the stadium, the thousands of people desperate and crying. It was something unexpected.

"Only three people have silenced the Maracanã – the Pope, Frank Sinatra and me."

↑ **Ghiggia celebrates scoring the winning goal for Uruguay in the 79th minute.**

So unexpected was the victory that Jules Rimet, the FIFA President, did not make a speech on handing the trophy over as he had only prepared one in Brazilian Portuguese.

"The game finished, I think at 4.45pm. We left the stadium at 8 o'clock at night, because we didn't know what could happen, how the Brazilian fans would take it. There was no security. We just left by ourselves.

"From there we went to the hotel, and there were a few Uruguayan people there who had been at the game. We celebrated with them. And we spent the night there. We were searching for the treasurer so that he could give us some money so that we could celebrate, but we never found him, so we had a collection between the players and we bought sandwiches and beers and went up to a room and celebrated there.

"We stayed in Brazil until the 18th because there wasn't enough space on the plane for us all, and we all wanted to travel together.

"Every year after that the team would get together on July 16 and have dinner with some invited guests. But then some of us started disappearing so we stopped. We don't do it anymore.

"The Brazil fans have been very kind to me but it hurt them. Years after the final, I flew to Rio and when I presented my identification and boarding pass, the girl – I think she was about 24 years old – kept turning my identification card over. I asked her whether there was a problem. She said, 'No, no, you are Ghiggia. The one from the Maracanã?' I said, 'Yes but that was a long time ago.' She gave me the card back and said, 'Yes, but it still hurts us here.'

"Now when I go to Brazil the papers say, 'The ghost of Maracanã has arrived.'"

Although he was considered a national hero, Ghiggia only ever played 12 times for Uruguay and only ever scored four goals, all during the 1950 FIFA World Cup™. After the tournament Ghiggia went to play in Italy for AS Roma and AC Milan and ultimately played for the Italian national team. He died in Montevideo in 2015, 65 years to the day after the 1950 final. He was the last surviving member of the 1950 Uruguayan team.

© FIFA TM

Edson Arantes
do Nascimento
PELÉ

TEAM	**Brazil**
BORN	**23 October 1940**
THE MATCH	**In 1958 the FIFA World Cup™ was hosted by Sweden. The final was played on 29 June in the Råsunda Solna Stadium.**
ATTENDANCE	**49,737**
RESULT	**Sweden 2-5 Brazil**
THE GOAL	**Pelé scored in the 55th and 90th minutes.**
PHOTOGRAPHED	**in São Paulo**

I n 1958 Brazil had never won the FIFA World Cup™. They had lost in 1954 to Hungary in the quarter-finals and were still haunted by their 1950 loss in the final to Uruguay. The name Pelé meant nothing – he was a 17-year-old kid, just signed to Santos FC two years previously.

"My father was a professional footballer, but he injured his knee which ended his career.

"I remember the 1950 World Cup when Brazil played at the Maracanã. I must have been about ten years old. My father and all his friends were preparing all this food for a big party because they were expecting to become champions. Brazil lost. My dad was crying, everyone was crying and only an hour before it had been a party. I was only ten so I couldn't understand. I said, 'Dad, why are you crying?' and he said, 'Because Brazil lost the World Cup.' To try to make him feel better I said, 'No, don't cry, I'm going to win the cup for you.'

"Five years later I was at Santos, a year after that I was in the national team, and a year after that I was in the World Cup Final.

"My mother hadn't wanted me to become a footballer because of what had happened with my dad. She said, 'No, you're not going to Santos, you're not leaving here because you have to become a teacher.'

"After the disappointments of '50 and '54 the Brazilian people really didn't have much confidence in the Brazilian team, I think.

Brazil has never had another team like the one in '58.

If you take player for player and compare them, still today I don't think there has been one better.

"For the first time ever the team had a psychologist – a man called Dr Cavalho. He said because I was only 17 I was too young to cope with the pressures of the World Cup and shouldn't be allowed to go. He also said Garrincha was too irresponsible and he shouldn't go either. What did he know!?"

Brazil topped their group and met Wales in the quarter-final. Pelé started this game and scored the only goal. In the semi-final, they faced France, who were considered one of the best teams in the world. Brazil won 5-2.

"I think there was more pressure on the older players. The morning of the final they were talking to all the journalists while I was playing dice with the children of the people who owned the hotel we were staying in. I remember they were all very blond, which was novel.

"The final was against Sweden, the host nation. We thought, 'Well, we're going to play the home nation, it's going to be a very tough game.' And it was the easiest game for us. We scored five.

↓ **Pelé scores Brazil's third goal past Swedish goalkeeper Svensson.**

"I was thinking, 'Could it be that my father is watching me in a World Cup?'"

"I was putting on my boots and thinking about my father and my mother in Bauru. I didn't know if they were listening or if they weren't because there was no television.

"Also, when the King of Sweden came down to the pitch to shake my hand, I was thinking, 'Gosh, do you think my father knows about this? Could he be listening? Is he listening there in Brazil?'

"It was a bit of a shock when they took the lead, but I remember Didi [Waldyr Pereira, the Brazilian midfielder] getting the ball from the back of the net and saying, 'Look, the game starts now. We're not going to worry.'

↑ **Pelé heads the ball into the goal to score Brazil's fifth and final goal of the 1958 final.**

"Vava scored our first and then I scored the *sombrero*. I took it on my chest, I played it over the top of the defender and I struck it as it came down. The ball came to my side, I stopped it, put it over the opponent and I scored the goal.

"And the last goal was a header where I jumped over my marker. I had a good take-off. The goalkeeper was following the action, which was with Zagallo. I ran into the area ... and I headed it in.

"I remember even the Swedish fans applauding Brazil. We were looking over at the reserves on the touchline waiting for the final whistle. And then it was a big party.

"Eight years before, in '50, I was telling my father 'Don't cry, I'll win a World Cup for you.' I started crying. Gilmar, who was the Santos goalkeeper at the time, came over and hugged me and he said, 'Stop crying, stop crying, boy!' But it was a very strong emotion that you can't explain – you can't describe what you feel.

"We're talking about the goals, the goals of the final, but the goal – going back a little – the goal against Wales, for me, was the most important goal of the Cup because it was my first goal and it was the goal that kept us in the World Cup. If I hadn't scored that goal, there would have been no final and Brazil's heart would have been broken again."

After the 1958 final Pelé's life would never be the same again. He is considered to be the greatest footballer of all time, and his name is synonymous with Brazilian football. Brazil would go on to dominate the FIFA World Cup™ Finals by winning it five times to date.

In 1999 Pelé was voted World Player of the Century by the International Federation of Football History & Statistics. That year, France Football asked their former Ballon d'Or winners to choose the Football Player of the Century. They chose Pelé. For more on Pelé, see pages 64-5.

1958

Mário ZAGALLO

TEAM	**Brazil**
BORN	**9 August 1931**
THE MATCH	**In 1958 the FIFA World Cup™ was hosted by Sweden. The final was played on 29 June in the Råsunda Solna Stadium.**
ATTENDANCE	**49,737**
RESULT	**Sweden 2-5 Brazil**
THE GOAL	**In the 68th minute Zagallo scored Brazil's fourth goal.**
PHOTOGRAPHED	**at home in Rio de Janeiro**

"**M**y father was against me playing football. He said it was like being a bum. I started playing in the streets, even playing with a stone if there was no football. Where the Maracanã is now, there used to be a track where they raced horses. It got knocked down and we played on the wasteland before they started to build the Maracanã."

In 1958 Brazil were still smarting from their defeat in the 1950 final to Uruguay in front of 200,000 home fans. They had failed to make an impression on the 1954 FIFA World Cup™ Finals, going out in the quarter-finals to the ultimate finalists, Hungary.

"In 1950, in the World Cup between Brazil and Uruguay, I was doing my military service. I was working as security around the pitch, wearing [an] olive-green helmet, truncheon and boots, watching the final. It was extraordinary. When Brazil came out to start the game there was a huge celebration in the Maracanã, with 200,000 people all waving white handkerchiefs. It was indescribable. Those handkerchiefs ended up being used to dry the tears that everyone shed.

"I could never have imagined that eight years later it would be me wearing the yellow shirt, and I would become World Cup champion ...

↓ Zagallo scores Brazil's second in the 68th minute.

but that's what the Gods decided and there I was ... in the final!"

Brazil comfortably topped their group and beat Wales in the quarter-final. In the semi-final against France, the match was even at 1-1 when the French captain, and their most experienced defender, Robert Jonquet, broke his leg at 36 minutes, leaving the French with ten men. As no substitutes were allowed then, the Brazilians took control and a Pelé hat-trick saw them into the final.

"I remember we were out training one day, just by the hotel. The others had run on ahead and Paulo Amaral, our coach, said to me, 'Let's go for a run down here.' I was wearing some new training boots and one of the studs came off. I made a deal with myself, 'If I find that stud from my boot on my way back, we'll be World Cup champions.' It was a pebble dirt track so the chances were almost nil, but on the way back I found it. We would become world champions!

"The directors of the Swedish confederation knew we weren't used to playing in the rain. The pitches played very differently if they were dry. So what did they do? It was raining Friday and Saturday, but on Sunday it improved. Other countries could have used this to their advantage, but when it started to rain they covered the pitch with a waterproof canvas so the pitch would be dry on the day of the final. We were so grateful for this kindness. They really didn't have to do it.

"The night before the final was an anxious time. Didi was smoking. In the dark, all I could see was the end of his cigar burning. He was anxious. He couldn't sleep. Even the guys who didn't smoke were smoking too. It was a time to get rid of our inner demons.

"The opposition, Sweden, played in yellow shirts, so we, the visitors, Brazil, could not play in yellow too. We weren't prepared for this. We had to have our badges sewn onto blue shirts for the match. There were some people who thought playing in blue was bad luck because we had not played in it much. Paulo Machado de Carvalho, our manager, said it was the robe of Our Lady, that she would bring us good luck, and that put the guys' minds to rest.

"We conceded a goal in the first five minutes. Didi went over slowly to pick the ball out of the net, tucking it underneath his arm. It was like watching a movie in slow motion. When he got to the centre circle, I ran over, saying, 'Come on, quick, we're losing the game.' But he knew what needed doing. He was showing them we weren't flustered, we were in control and we were going to get back in the game. And he was right."

Within five minutes Brazil had equalised, with the genius of Garrincha setting up Vavá, who scored again 23 minutes later. The 17-year-old newcomer, Pelé, put the match beyond the Swedes in the 55th minute, flicking the ball over the defenders' heads to volley one of the greatest FIFA World Cup™ goals of all time, and announce his arrival the world stage. From then on, the Brazilians began to enjoy themselves.

"The fourth goal was my goal. It was a corner kick, the defender headed it, the ball fell to Didi's feet and he took it badly. The ball landed at my feet and I went over the defender. We were leg against leg with the ball, but the ball stayed with me. He should have won it because he was much stronger, but somehow I kept the ball.

↑ **Brazil celebrate their first World Cup victory, holding the Swedish flag to acknowledge the support they received from the crowd in Stockholm.**

I was in front of the keeper. It went under him and into the left corner.

"At the end, the referee had the ball. He was holding the ball here, like this, under his arm. Paolo Machado de Carvalho said he'd like to have the ball as a trophy. Mário Américo, our masseur, wasted no time. He went on to the pitch. The referee had the ball like this, under one arm, and he gave it a tap, got the ball and off he ran to the changing room. We were all there celebrating and the referee came in wanting the ball. So they gave him another ball. He got a ball, but the real ball stayed with Paulo Machado de Carvalho."

Zagallo's place in Brazil's World Cup history is unique.
He was involved in seven FIFA World Cup™ campaigns.
He scored in the 1958 final. He played in the 1962 final,
winning again. He was the manager of, arguably, the
greatest team ever, in 1970 and also in 1974. He was
assistant manager in 1994, coach in 1998 and technical
director in 2006. Of his achievements, he says:

"I have more medals than any other Brazilian. They
made a statue of me to put up in the Maracanã. I don't
know where it is. I think they'll put it up when I'm dead,
which is no use to me. The important thing is that I'm
still here!"

Retired, Zagallo lives in Rio de Janeiro.

1962

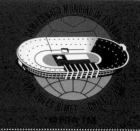

Josef
MASOPUST

TEAM	**Czechoslovakia**
BORN	**9 February 1931–29 June 2015**
THE MATCH	**In 1962 the FIFA World Cup was hosted by Chile. The Final was played on 17 June in the Estadio Nacional, Santiago.**
ATTENDANCE	**68,679**
RESULT	**Brazil 3-1 Czechoslovakia**
THE GOAL	**In the 15th minute Masopust scored for Czechoslovakia.**
PHOTOGRAPHED	**at Dukla Praha's home ground, Stadion Juliska, Prague**

The country of Czechoslovakia was created in 1918 in the wake of the First World War. It remained a democracy until March 1939 when Hitler invaded at the beginning of the Second World War. The Nazis ruled with an iron fist until September 1944 when it was liberated by the Red Army of the Soviet Union. Under the influence of Soviet Russia, it would remain a communist state behind the "iron curtain" until 1989.

Czechoslovakia had qualified for the 1958 FIFA World Cup™ Finals in Sweden but had failed to get out of the group stages. In spite of that experience, the expectations of the national team in 1962 were low. They managed to scrape out of the group stages only to meet neighbours Hungary and Yugoslavia in the quarter- and semi-finals.

"I was born in Most [now Czech Republic] in the north of Czechoslovakia in 1931. I was one of six boys. My father was a coal miner. He supported me being a footballer provided, he said, I gave it 100 per cent. When I started playing, we were still occupied by the Germans, so it was only Germans who could play in teams. It wasn't until after the war that I could join a team. I joined Teplice but after two years I had to do my military service. That's how I joined Dukla Praha, which was the army team. I stayed with them until the end of my career. We didn't get paid as such; we just got our army wages.

"When we qualified in 1962 people were telling us, 'When you get there, don't even bother unpacking because you'll be coming back straight away.' Even when we were leaving for Chile, no one came to wish us good luck or anything.

"Each country had to sort out their own accommodation. Because we were communist, we had the cheapest accommodation that no one else wanted. When we would travel back to our hotel each day, the local people in the village would shout, "*Checo, checo!*" in the street, because they knew no one else had wanted to stay there. They welcomed us and made us feel very at home."

Czechoslovakia would eventually meet Brazil in the final, but first they had to play them in the group stages.

"For the match against Brazil we had a simple tactic, which was to do everything not to lose.

↓ **Masopust shoots the ball past Brazilian goalkeeper Gilmar to score the first goal of the 1962 final.**

"This was the match in which Pelé pulled a muscle, which ended this World Cup for him. There was no such thing as substitutes then, so he had to stay on. At one point he had the ball on the wing. I ran in to close him down. I was going to finish him off but when I was about a metre and a half away I saw he was injured so I pulled up so I wouldn't make things worse for him. When he saw this he kicked the ball into touch.

"The day of the final was special for me, not only because I was about to play in the World Cup Final, but also because it was my wife's birthday. So, I would have the chance to celebrate two things that day if it worked out. (Sadly, I wasn't able to celebrate either of them, as my wife wasn't with us because one family member always had to stay at home so that the other wouldn't defect. They were scared that if the whole family went abroad they would stay there and never come back.)

"Before every match, we would be in the changing room for an hour and a half to prepare in a calm manner. But when we arrived at the stadium there were lots of journalists and reporters. They gave an award for the best goalkeeper of the tournament to Vilda Schrojf, so the dressing room was full and we couldn't prepare properly. I have to be honest and say that we didn't really believe we could win against Brazil. We knew the quality of their squad and we didn't really believe it. I stretched and tied my boots properly, which I did about two or three times before I did it right. Only when we went out in the tunnel, did we hear the noise and the atmosphere ahead.

"We were attacking on the left wing. I was running into the box and I saw a gap in the defence. I got given a beautiful ball, so I just hit it in the net. I was happy.

↑ **Masopust playing; his goal was Czechoslovakia's only goal in the final.**

"It had been a dream since I was a little boy to score a goal in the World Cup Final.

"But before I could comprehend the joy I should have been feeling, they scored and ruined it for me. Amarildo, who was playing instead of Pelé, crossed the ball from the left, and our keeper, who'd made no mistakes the whole tournament, came out for the cross, misjudged it and it went in, right behind his back.

"It was 1-1 at half-time, and we thought we had a chance of playing for a win and started out well in the second half. It was an even game, but Amarildo again crossed the ball and Zito finished it with his head. Brazil showed their superiority by scoring three goals. We felt we'd done our best, but Brazil were just the better team. We really had no grudges after the match.

"We didn't know what to expect when we got home because no one had cared when we left. We were curious to see what kind of reception we'd get when we arrived in Prague. It had changed 100 per cent. We could hardly get through customs. It was crazy. After that, though, I think our lifestyle was pretty much the same as before. From the fans' point of view it was a huge success, but officially not really. We only got 5,000 Czech crowns [USD 180], from which they wanted taxes. We were quite disappointed.

VJEZD
POUZE
NA
POVOLENÍ

Masopust was awarded European Footballer of the Year in 1962. He retired from international football in 1966 when Czechoslovakia failed to qualify for the FIFA World Cup™ Finals in England. However, as a reward for his services he was allowed to move abroad, working first in Indonesia and then in Belgium. He returned to Prague to his original army flat in the shadow of the Dukla Praha stadium, where he died in 2015.

1962

AMARILDO
Tavares da Silveira

TEAM	**Brazil**
BORN	**born 29 July 1940**
THE MATCH	**In 1962 the FIFA World Cup™ was hosted by Chile. The final was played on 17 June in the Estadio Nacional, Santiago.**
ATTENDANCE	**68,679**
RESULT	**Brazil 3-1 Czechoslovakia**
THE GOAL	**Amarildo scored the equaliser for Brazil in the 17th minute.**
PHOTOGRAPHED	**at Botafogo Football Club, Rio de Janeiro**

"**M**y earliest memory is the 1950 World Cup – Brazil's defeat to Uruguay, here in Rio. I was 11 years old. It really stuck with me because it was like a funeral here in the whole of Brazil."

Amarildo began his career at Flamengo, but it was his move to Botafogo in 1960 that drew him to the attention of the national team.

Brazil came to Chile as favourites and reigning world champions having defeated Sweden in 1958. Pelé and Garrincha had made their mark in 1958 but, now four years older, they were arguably the two best players in the world. Brazil comfortably saw off Mexico 2-0 in their opening match, but disaster struck in their second match, a gruelling 0-0 draw with ultimate finalists Czechoslovakia, when Pelé got injured. He would not feature again in that FIFA World Cup™. Amarildo had the unenviable task of taking his place. In their last group game against Spain, Amarildo proved himself, scoring twice to beat Spain 2-0.

In the knockout stages, to reach the final Brazil beat England 3-1 and hosts Chile 4-2 and, although it did not matter, Amarildo failed to score in either match.

"The final was interesting because we'd already met Czechoslovakia at the start, in the second qualifying game in Viña del Mar. It was a very tough game, a 0-0 draw, and Pelé got injured. He was considered irreplaceable by just about everyone. Without him, the Brazilian people lost a bit of hope that we could win anything. But they forgot that we also had the likes of Garrincha, Didi, Zagallo, Nílton Santos and other really great players. And then there was me. Pelé was considered irreplaceable ... so I was to be the replacement for the irreplaceable.

"Running out onto the pitch is a very special moment because you completely transform.

"It doesn't happen in the changing room because there you're all together talking and chatting. It's when you leave the changing room you start to really think about the responsibility you have in a match like that. As a team you are all together, but you are alone in your thoughts.

"When we came out onto the pitch, the Czechs were there. I looked at them, but there were no smiles, no niceties, no shaking hands. We came on, we were over here, they were over there and it was like that until kick-off.

"We conceded the first goal after just 15 minutes. Masopust scored. We could have panicked, but Didi was there for us. He calmed us all down because he said, 'It's no problem. There's still a lot of time to play.'

"After the group stages were finished, in Viña del Mar, we had gone to watch the Czechoslovakia game against Mexico. Their goalkeeper, Schrojf – every time the Mexican wingers came down the wing to cross, he always came off his line to intercept the ball. He did this four or five times. Paulo Amaral [the Brazilian physio], said, "Look, Amarildo, the keeper always comes out before they cross the ball."

↓ Amarildo takes on the Czech defence while the game is still a tie.

It didn't seem like a big thing at the time but I must have made a mental note of it.

"So, in the final, just two minutes after Masopust's goal, Zagallo comes charging through for the cross. I dribbled through the two defenders and looked to see where he was. When I stopped to cross, he [Schrojf] had already come out off his line. So there it was: in a flash I remembered what Amaral had said, 'He's going to come out now.' I was already thinking it and, sure enough, he came out leaving enough space behind him for me to shoot. I shot and scored the goal. It can be just a small detail that can decide a championship but that's how it happened.

"Normally when I'd score I'd jump in the air but I didn't get a chance. It felt like the whole team, including Amaral, were on top of me.

↑ **Brazil equalise with Amarildo's free kick.**

I was completely buried under a mountain of players before I got the chance to celebrate.

"It was good we didn't let Czechoslovakia celebrate their goal much. So when after two minutes we equalised, we broke their spirits a little and took control of the game.

"In the second half I did exactly the same thing, dribbling down the wing, but this time Schrojf, remembering my goal, stuck to the near post, staying on his line. I saw this, pulled back a little, crossed it to Zito and he headed into an empty net. Ten minutes later Vavá scored and then it was like a big party.

"The celebrations weren't like they are today. There was nothing prepared – it was just the handing over of the cup. There was no stage; there was no kind of party like there is now. It was very simple but very genuine. It would be odd now but it was just right for the time. We were just looking at each other, hugging, saying, 'We did it!'

"Of course, it transformed my life but I hope it was also down to my own merits. Imagine if, when I replaced Pelé, things hadn't gone so well – what would have become of me?"

After the success of 1962 Amarildo went to play in Italy for AC Milan and ACF Fiorentina. He won one Coppa Italia in 1967 with Milan, and the Italian title ("Scudetto") in 1969 with Fiorentina. After a brief spell at Roma, his playing career ended in 1974. A number of botched operations on his legs has left him with a permanent disfigurement.

In 1984 he became manager at Espérance Sportive de Tunis in Tunisia, winning the Tunisian Championship in 1985 and the Tunisian Cup a year later. He moved to the United Arab Emirates to coach Al Ain FC. Amarildo won another league championship in the United Arab Emirates in 1993. In 2008 Amarildo was hired as América's head coach. In his first match, Volta Redonda FC beat América 4-2 and his contract was terminated a week later. He now lives in Rio de Janeiro.

© FIFA TM

José Ely de Miranda
ZITO

TEAM	**Brazil**
BORN	**8 August 1932–14 June 2015**
THE MATCH	**In 1962 the FIFA World Cup™ was hosted by Chile. The final was played on 17 June in the Estadio Nacional, Santiago.**
ATTENDANCE	**68,679**
RESULT	**Brazil 3-1 Czechoslovakia**
THE GOAL	**Zito scored Brazil's third goal in the 69th minute.**
PHOTOGRAPHED	**at Santos FC grounds**

A massive earthquake in Chile in 1960 did significant damage to the country's infrastructure including the host's stadiums. The country would struggle to be ready for the finals two years later. "Because we have nothing, we will give everything" became the unofficial slogan for the tournament.

Brazil came to the tournament as FIFA World Cup™ holders and favourites. Zito's nickname among the media was Gerente ("The Manager") because of the managerial role he seemed to take on the pitch.

"My earliest memory in football was the shocking 1950 Cup final – Brazil's defeat to Uruguay ... it was like the whole of Brazil was sad ... No one spoke. In those days we used to listen to the Cup final on the radio. It was even worse because we couldn't see anything.

"I came from a tiny village. On Wednesdays, from time to time, there was an ox sold in the village and we'd go to the butcher to get the ox's bladder, and we'd blow it up and it would become our ball. It wasn't quite round but it was a ball nevertheless. All the boys would play in the streets. It lasted for as long as it lasted, until it got a hole. Once it got a hole, that was it!

"I was at Santos [FC]. I lived there at the training camp. It was like a little hotel. Then Pelé arrived. He was very much a boy. He came here when he was only 14 or 15. He grew up here.

↓ **Zito heads Brazil's third goal in the 69th minute.**

"I was the team captain. I was very demanding and tough.

When we were hungry we'd send him to buy sandwiches. We'd let him keep the change. We sent him to buy drinks. He would make a list of all the things to do. He was still a child.

"When it was time for the call-ups [for the national team], we were all glued to the radio to find out if we would get a call-up or not. I was in great form at that time and received a call-up to go and train with the national team. This was the biggest news I received in my life.

"We had two players who could play against anyone. There was Garrincha, for whom, I think, 1962 was his greatest World Cup, and Amarildo, who took Pelé's place. He, too, was an excellent player, so we had it in our minds that we could reach the final.

"We knew the Czechoslovakia team. We had already played them in the group stages, when Pelé got injured."

Brazil came comfortably out of the group stages but then had to see off England, who would be the 1966 FIFA World Cup™ champions, and then hosted Chile in the semi-finals. In the Chile match, Garrincha, having been kicked and spat on for most of the game, got sent off for kicking Chile's Eladio Rojas. This would rule him out of the final. With Pelé already missing, this would have potentially spelled disaster for Brazil. However, after reviewing the footage, FIFA overruled the red card and allowed Garrincha to play in the final.

"In the morning, before the game, before lunch, we always had a general meeting of the whole group, and the coach and all the trainers all spoke. They would draw our attention to this and that. The coach would draw on the board the formation he wanted us all to play. But later he'd take each one of us aside. He'd give us a little pointer or ask us to do something. He gave me a lot of instructions because I was in the midfield so I could talk to everyone up front and at the back, so my job was almost that of a captain.

"Before going onto the field we would all embrace and have our little prayer. The Brazilians are like that, so we did our little prayer before going out onto the field.

"The adrenaline! Until you step onto the pitch, you are buzzing. But as soon as you step on the pitch it vanishes, you calm down. Each one of us knows what we're going to do and you just want the game to start.

"We conceded an early goal to Czechoslovakia, and it was an alarm bell for us. 'They're not such fools when it comes to football!' It was an alarm bell but we came back quickly with an answer. Amarildo's goal was quick.

"And then I scored the goal that decided the match. It seemed as though the goal had almost been planned because I was defending in our area, and when Brazil got the ball I got it and I passed it to Zagallo over on the left and I started to make a run towards Czechoslovakia's goal. I stayed with Zagallo. I was still in the middle of the field ... I stayed with the ball. I was shouting to him that Amarildo was up ahead of him.

↑ **Zito turns to the fans to celebrate.**

'Look, Amarildo! Amarildo!'

"I kept running. When I reached the goal area, Amarildo got the ball from Zagallo. He dribbled towards the Czech full-back and crossed it, because I was shouting, shouting, shouting.

"He crossed it and I was there practically on my own and headed it and scored.

"It was an easy goal to score.

"Everyone jumped on top of me. I had the ten of them on top of me. I fell over and was on the floor, celebrating!

"Vavá's goal was funny because the Czech goalkeeper was voted the best goalkeeper of the tournament. Djalma Santos who was our right wing, booted the ball forwards from the midfield. The ball came high and the Czech goalkeeper, Schrojf, came to get the ball and, when he grabbed it, it hit his chest and bounced back, and Vavá, who was standing right next to him, just touched the ball and scored. It was the easiest goal he scored in his life. The goalkeeper almost passed it to him. It was so simple.

"When we got the third goal we felt like champions, second-time World Cup champions, because there was no way we could lose the game. It was a party. We were invaded by Brazilians. The changing room could take 30 people – 300 came in there.

"Going back home was amazing, too. They put us on a fire engine. And they took us from the airport to the Federação Paulista de Futebol [the organisation that manages football tournaments in São Paolo]. We passed through the city on the top of a fire engine, celebrating.

"This goal didn't change my professional life because my professional life was already stable. But for my ego it was the victory goal. A goal is a goal but it was the most important goal of my life."

Zito remained in a mentoring role to the young Pelé. They would later become business partners with mixed degrees of success. He was offered lucrative deals to move abroad, particularly to Italy, but he chose to remain at Santos for the entirety of his career. He never took on a managerial role but took various backroom roles including scouting and youth development. As a scout, he discovered future stars Robinho and an 11-year-old Neymar. He passed away on 14 June 2015.

1966

© FIFA TM

Sir Geoff
HURST

TEAM	**England**
BORN	**8 December 1941**
THE MATCH	**In 1966 the FIFA World Cup™ was hosted by England. The final was played on 30 July in Wembley Stadium, London.**
ATTENDANCE	**96,924**
RESULT	**England 4-2 West Germany after extra time**
THE GOAL	**Hurst scored in the 18th, 101st and 120th minutes.**
PHOTOGRAPHED	**at Hendon Hall Hotel, where the team had stayed the night before the final**

England came to the 1966 finals as hosts but not favourites. A lot of England's hopes rested on the shoulders of Tottenham Hotspur striker and England's top scorer Jimmy Greaves. After a bumpy start against Uruguay, England topped their group with relative ease, but Greaves – who refused to wear shinpads as he thought they slowed him down – suffered a gash on his leg that required 14 stitches. Greaves was left out of the infamous quarter-final against Argentina.

In March 1966, just months before the first match would kick-off, the Jules Rimet Trophy was stolen, causing huge embarrassment to the English Football Association. The trophy was found by a dog named Pickles two weeks later, at the bottom of a garden in South London, wrapped in newspaper.

In spite of a disappointing draw with Uruguay in the opening match, England came out of the group stages with ease. They faced Argentina in the quarter-final, which is regarded as one of the most brutal matches in football history. In contrast, the semi-final against Eusébio's Portugal was a display of brilliance and gentlemanly behaviour.

"I was surprised that Sir Alf [Alfred Ramsey, England manager 1963–74] picked me for England. I still am today. Two years before I was a struggling midfield player who could hardly get a game for West Ham. Fans used to write to me asking me to get Bobby Moore's autograph for them. I just wasn't on the radar until I got a letter saying I'd been selected to play in the friendly against Poland in December 1965. I didn't play in that game but must have made an impression in training.

"I was on the bench for the Uruguay game. It was disappointing we didn't win but I remember just being glad to be there. I hadn't deserved to start because I hadn't played so well in a couple of games.

"Jimmy [Greaves] damaged his shin in the France game. He wasn't just world-class, he was one in a whole generation. I was lucky.

"That's how I made my debut in the quarter-final against Argentina. That game was tough. We were under no illusions. We knew it was going to be aggressive.

"The win was satisfying. We'd won and I'd scored but I was thinking if Jimmy was fit I still wouldn't be in."

The match was so brutal that Sir Alf Ramsey ran on the pitch at full time and refused to let the England players swap shirts with the Argentines, describing them as "animals". The German referee, Rudolf Kreitlein, had to have a police escort from the pitch for his own safety.

Hurst played well in the semi-final win against Portugal but did not score.

"The night before the final we all went to the cinema. Alf told each player individually whether they were playing or not. I still wasn't sure about me, but he took me aside – I honestly can't remember where exactly – and told me I was playing. He said,

'You're playing tomorrow. Keep your mouth shut, don't tell anybody.'

"I had known Martin [Peters] since we were kids at West Ham. It was impossible to keep our mouths shut – we were sharing a room – so by bedtime we knew we were both playing.

↑ **Hurst heads the equaliser for England in the 18th minute.**

"I had a good night's sleep. I would have had a good night's sleep whether I was playing or not. I didn't wake early, about 9.30am, and my first thought was to see what the weather was like to decide which studs to wear later. It was wet, grey and drizzling so I decided to wear nylon instead of rubber studs. I got up, popped out to get a paper and went for a walk around the grounds. There were other people staying at the hotel. Nothing was cordoned off.

"When we got to Wembley, the changing room was pandemonium. There was all the committee members and lots of people I'd never seen in my life before. There was a guy from Wembley handing out teas.

"What's significant about the tunnel was, the moment you get out there, right at the bottom from the dressing rooms, and look up, you hear [the roar of the crowd] immediately. Within seconds somebody at the top of the tunnel knows we're out, he's telling somebody else and … it's like a fire, and that's when you really start … Wow! … The hairs on your neck are standing up already.

↑ **Wolfgang Weber looks on as Hurst's controversial goal bounces out of the net in the 101st minute.**

"As you're walking up the tunnel I just felt the whole country was up there.

It's not a football match when you get this far, it's a national event and everybody ... *everybody*'s involved.

"They've gone a goal up; we're going to get it back. Not once did we think, particularly that early on, that we were in any sort of trouble. A weaker team could have let it get to them.

"Our first goal was like something from the training ground. At West Ham we were conditioned to take throw-ins, corner kicks and free kicks very quickly. It just became a habit. If there was something on then, split, you do it. It's the same whether it's on the training

ground, for England or in the World Cup Final. It's very satisfying taking something from the training ground to the World Cup Final. Bobby [Moore] won the free kick. You can see him looking up. He takes it very quickly. I'd already flattened the goalkeeper earlier on so he wasn't going to come out and get involved. You could get away with a bit more then, so Hans Tilkowski was still on his line, and I scored the goal."

The match remained tied at 1-1 at half-time.

"I can't remember a word anyone said at half-time. To be honest, I can't remember half-time at all."

Martin Peters, Hurst's West Ham team-mate, scored what would have been the winner in the 78th minute but the West Germans equalised in the 90th minute, forcing the match into extra time.

"I thought the disputed goal for me technically was a good goal. I've always believed it was in. It was a very difficult cross from Alan Ball. I had to take a couple of touches to get it back on line and hit it on the half-turn."

This second goal of Hurst's and England's third in the 101st minute is the most disputed goal in football history. There was no dispute about his equally famous third goal in the closing seconds of the match.

"Another great thing about Bobby was his ability to hit the ball from defence to attack. As I'm going to the edge of the box, I'm thinking 'I'm going to hit this now with my left foot. The game's nearly finished and, if it goes beyond the goal into the crowd, by the time the ball-boy gets it to Tilkowski the German keeper, the game's got to be over.'

I mis-hit it and it flew in."

This made Hurst the only player ever to have scored three times in a FIFA World Cup™ Final. The BBC commentator Kenneth Wolstenholme's description of the match's closing moments has gone down in history: "And here comes Hurst. He's got ... Some people are on the pitch, they think it's all over – it is now! It's four!"

"The next morning, I picked up the national newspaper, front page of a national newspaper, and it said: 'England Win World Cup – See back page.' ... Astounding."

Hurst is still the only person to have scored a hat-trick in a FIFA World Cup™ Final.
He stayed at West Ham until 1972 when he signed for Stoke City. After spells at West
Bromwich Albion and the Seattle Sounders he retired from playing. His managerial
career was brief, with stints at Chelsea and Kuwait SC. He left football in 1984 to
become an insurance salesman. He initially struggled with such attitudes summed up in
comments like "I don't deal with footballers" but did carve out a very successful career
in sales before retiring in 2002. He was awarded a knighthood in 1998. He lives in
Chelmsford with his wife Judith.

1966

© FIFA TM

PETERS

Sir Alf Ramsey, the England manager, had declared on his appointment in 1962 that England would win the next FIFA World Cup™. He seemed alone in his thinking. Martin Peters formed part of the West Ham United trio with Bobby Moore and Geoff Hurst that would leave an indelible mark on the '66 FIFA World Cup™. Described by Sir Alf Ramsey as being "ten years ahead of his time", Peters had played in every position for West Ham, including goalkeeper.

"My dad was a Thames lighterman [barge worker on the Thames in London], a job which was passed down from father to son, and he told me that he would like me to go on the river, too. I was playing for Dagenham Schoolboys. A scout came round our house from Fulham and said to my dad, 'Is it possible for Martin to come to Fulham?' My dad said, 'Well, if you're not going to be a Thames lighterman, then I think West Ham's the best club.' I always took notice of what my dad said, so we had a meeting with Ted Fenton [West Ham manager 1950-61] and that was it – I signed on the dotted line.

"I got a letter from the FA saying I'd been picked as part of the squad for the friendly game at Wembley against Yugoslavia. The letter said I'd be paid a penny a mile for my travel expenses to Wembley. We won 2-0. Alf Ramsey seemed pleased with the way I played.

"There was an initial squad of 27 names to go to Lilleshall [the England training camp] About three weeks later, Alf called us into a room and said he was going to name the 22 players to go to the World Cup Finals. You can imagine what it was like.

↓ **Peters scores to give England the lead in the 78th minute.**

Everyone's biting their nails or whatever, and suddenly he calls number 16 – he calls my name out.

It was an unbelievable feeling. I was going to be part and parcel of the World Cup.

"We got to the quarter-finals. Unfortunately for Jimmy [Greaves], he got injured. He wouldn't wear pads, because he didn't run as well with the pads on. He got a bad gash down his shin, which, if he had had pads on, he might have survived, but he didn't, and it gave Geoff [Hurst] the opportunity to come in and Alf changed the way we played completely.

"Alf wasn't unlike Capello really, in that he was very strict. He used to come in, we had our own room in the Hendon Hall Hotel, and we'd be watching the television. Ten o'clock and he'd come in and say, 'Goodnight, gentlemen,' and that was it, we went to bed! And that was it; so that's how he was.

"It wasn't till the night before [the final], we went to the cinema – there was 22 players plus about four or five others, like Alf Ramsey and Harold Shepherdson [England assistant manager] and the other guys with us. Can you imagine that happening now, about 24 or 25 of us walking down the road going to the cinema? They wouldn't get away with it. *Those Magnificent Men in Their Flying Machines* was what I think we saw, and it was in the reception area, Alf Ramsey came up to me and said, 'Martin, you're playing tomorrow.' Only he said, 'Keep it to yourself,' so I kept it to myself. Then we went back to the room. Geoff looked at me, I looked at him and he said,

'Are you in?' And I said, 'Yeah!'

So we were both in.

"The morning of the final we didn't have to go down for breakfast if we didn't want to so we could just relax. Nobby Stiles being a Catholic was quite keen to go to church. Hendon Hall, our hotel, was in a Jewish area so he went out to look for a church and couldn't find anywhere. I think he said a little prayer outside the hotel and just came back.

"We went down for lunch, had a meeting with Alf and then next thing you're up in your room putting your grey suit, FA tie and brand-new shirt on. I thought, 'This is it.' When we came out of the hotel there were hundreds of people. We had a police escort. About a mile down the road there was a fire station and all the lads were out of the station waving flags and wishing us luck. That meant so much to all of us.

↑ **Peters celebrates what would have been the winning goal, until West Germany scored in the 90th minute.**

"It was a typical English summer's day – it rained.

"There was a guy who bought tickets off the players, offering quite a lot of money for them and I sold my two tickets that we were allowed to have, to this guy and like a fool I made a big mistake because it meant my mum and dad couldn't go. So I really regret that even today – I feel embarrassed by it, just telling you about it.

"Coming out of the tunnel with almost 100,000 people and you're walking side by side with the West Germans, the noise was just chilling. After about 15 minutes, the worst thing happened, we conceded a goal. Then Geoff had a great header and we equalised. It was important we went into half-time 1-1.

"Bally [Alan Ball], took the corner and I don't know how he got it to the far post but it went out to the far post, out of the penalty area where Geoff Hurst was standing and I don't know why Geoff, why he stood there to be honest with you, but the ball went to Geoff and really instead of looking up to pass he kind of pushed it to one side and had a shot. Fortunately it wasn't a very good shot. I'd pulled off a bit about two to three yards outside the penalty box and I could see the ball coming and I thought, 'God, it's coming to me!'

It hit the back of the net and ... it was wild, it was just wild."

After Peter scored what would have been the winning goal there were still 13 minutes to play. In the 90th minute Wolfgang Weber scored for West Germany.

"We kicked and off the referee blew the whistle for the end of the game. We were seconds, literally seconds away from winning it. Alf came on and we gathered in the centre circle. Bobby Moore sat down and Alf said, 'Get up. Show 'em how strong you are, show 'em you're not weak, look at the Germans there over there having their legs massaged, they're lying all over the place, you're standing up. You've won it once. Now go and win it again!'"

Geoff Hurst famously scored twice in extra time to secure England's only FIFA World Cup™.

"I was only 22; Bally was only 20 – he was the youngest. So very young for me, and I think in your mind when you settle down you think, well, maybe we can win it again, but now we're 40-odd years on we still haven't."

Peters moved to Tottenham Hotspur in 1970 for a record-breaking GBP 200,000 where he stayed until he moved to Norwich City FC. He finished his playing career at Sheffield United. In 1984 he followed his 1966 team-mate Geoff Hurst into insurance sales a job he did until his retirement in 2001. He has been married to his wife, Kathleen, since 1964 and has two children and two grandchildren.

1966

Wolfgang

WEBER

TEAM	**West Germany**
BORN	**26 June 1944**
THE MATCH	**In 1966 the FIFA World Cup™ was hosted by England. The final was played on 30 July in Wembley Stadium, London.**
ATTENDANCE	**96,924**
RESULT	**England 4-2 West Germany after extra time**
THE GOAL	**In the 89th minute Weber scored for West Germany to take the match into extra time.**
PHOTOGRAPHED	**at Porz Sports Club, Cologne**

Weber was born in Porz, Cologne, and played for his local club from the age of ten. He joined FC Cologne and was selected for the national team aged 19. After West Germany only reached the quarter-finals in 1962, they set about reorganising the structure of German football. The national coach, Josef "Sepp" Herberger, who had been in the job for 28 years was replaced by Helmut Schön, who became West Germany's most successful manager.

"In March 1965, during the European Cup match in Rotterdam, I injured myself – I broke my fibula. This should have been a disaster but I still managed to get fit for the World Cup. I was only 22. Franz Beckenbauer and I were the youngest.

"The atmosphere among the team was brilliant. We had a group of very experienced players – a middle-aged group – and a group of very young players – Franz Beckenbauer, Wolfgang Overath, Horst-Dieter Höttges and me.

"We had a warm welcome in England. We came out of the groups well. If you win two out of three matches and one ends in a draw, obviously the mood was getting better and better during the tournament.

"We weren't so much welcome in the final, though. For the semi-final we had to go to Liverpool, to Goodison Park and play the Soviet Union with the legendary Lev Yashin as goalkeeper. We won that match 2-1 and then it was on to London for the final.

"It is particularly difficult to play against the host country, because the majority of the crowd is all supporting the home team.

"We were very well prepared, and in the evening before going to bed we had a small bottle of beer. Me being a young player, I would have never thought that we might lose the match.

"Tactically, we were all set the day before. I knew that I was going to play against Roger Hunt [England forward]. I didn't have to think about him too much as I had played against him three times before, in the European Cup, against Liverpool. We're still good friends today.

"It was a big day – 98,000 people in the Wembley Stadium. All of London had gone totally mad. The English fans were showing us the thumbs-down, but you just deal with it.

"When we got into the changing rooms at Wembley, there was a weird minty smell. It must have been there from the team before, but it was everywhere we went in England. I think it must have been a massage oil or something.

We walked onto the pitch from the tunnel; I had shivers down my spine.

↓ **Weber sees off an England attack.**

The noise was deafening. We could sometimes hear some German fans but mostly they got drowned out.

"The match started up with trying to get a feel for each other – both teams were playing for safety. We managed to take the lead quite early after just 15 minutes due to an English defensive error. Gordon Banks [England's goalkeeper] had no chance. If you can take the lead, you of course think you can win the match.

"But, unfortunately, the English managed to level things up at 1-1 after a free kick, due to some misunderstandings in our defence. It all happened very quickly. I think it was a header by Geoff Hurst.

"It was 1-1 at half-time and we still thought we could win the match. There were no substitutes, so there were no tactical changes to be made.

"The only thing I can remember about England's second goal is that there was a ricochet and suddenly there was Martin Peters all on his own by our goalkeeper and he buried the ball in the net.

"With ten minutes to go we still hadn't scored. You are aware of the time available getting smaller and smaller.

"Just before the end we got a free kick. From the bench, Helmut Schön and Dettmar Cramer signalled to us that that this would be it if we didn't score, because time was running out. And so we just shouted, 'Everyone upfield, everyone upfield!'

"I was far upfield anyway. Lothar Emmerich's free kick hit the wall and bounced back and touched [Karl-Heinz] Schnellinger's hip, and suddenly, between hundreds of legs – I only saw legs – the ball was lying in front of me. I thought, 'I have to put it in the net quickly, before the referee blows the final whistle.'

"I curled it exactly in the corner I was aiming for.

The referee did blow the whistle, but it wasn't for time, it was for the goal. We were back in it.

"Extra time was incredibly exhausting. Certainly, our passing wasn't ideal, and Willi Schulz suddenly had to face Geoff Hurst, and Hurst, out of the turn, did a fantastic shot in the direction of the goal. I was right there. The ball bounced and I headed it over for a corner. Unfortunately for us it wasn't like that. The assistant referee had noticed the English reaction – they all had their hands in the air hands in the air and thought the ball must be in the net. You can see me on TV pulling down Bobby Charlton's hands, so that the assistant referee wouldn't take any other decision than to continue the match. But the [third] goal was given.

↑ **Weber (left) clinches the equaliser in the last minute of ordinary time.**

"We were exhausted. The Wembley pitch was heavy-going. Later on England dominated the game and they scored their fourth. We had lost control of the game, so England were the deserved World Cup champions, but the third goal wasn't a goal.

"The disappointment was huge but we felt we could leave with our heads held high. On the bus back to our hotel the English fans lined the streets and applauded us. We went out that night and had a few beers. We had been under so much pressure and now it was all over.

"When we arrived back in Frankfurt we hoped the German fans would forgive us but we were welcomed like World Champions. It was very moving."

Weber stayed at FC Cologne until his retirement in 1978 and is now involved with his first club, Porz, again.

1970

MEXICO 70 © TM FIFA

Edson Arantes do Nascimento
PELÉ

TEAM	Brazil
BORN	23 October 1940
THE MATCH	In 1970 the FIFA World Cup™ was hosted by Mexico. The final was played on 21 June in the Estadio Azteca, Mexico City.
ATTENDANCE	107,412
RESULT	Brazil 4-1 Italy
THE GOAL	In the 18th minute Pelé scored Brazil's first goal.
PHOTOGRAPHED	in São Paulo

Mexico was a controversial choice for the 1970 finals. The high altitude did not suit the players. This was exacerbated by the decision to play many of the matches, including the final, in the blistering midday heat, to cater for global television audiences. Although Brazil had won two of the previous three World Cups, they had gone out in the group stages in 1966 and a number of the team, including Pelé, were clearly in the twilight of their careers. The team assembled to go to Mexico, however, is considered the greatest football team of all time.

"In 1970 there were lots of pressures. There were problems with the government. Brazil had done badly at the World Cup in 1966. We had won in '58 and '62, but I got injured against Portugal in '66 and we went out. I wasn't sure whether to play again or not. I'd keep playing for Santos but I wasn't sure about the national team. Eventually, I decided to play and started getting ready.

"In the run-up to the '70 Cup, there were certain conflicts, certain problems with the coach, who was a journalist and had been placed as a coach. He was an interim called João Saldanha. The players didn't like him. He was replaced by [Mário] Zagallo.

"So there was a big controversy about this and at that point I said, 'Gosh, this is the last Cup, I'm going to have to say goodbye. I can't lose, I'm not going out as a loser.' There were about four or five of us for whom it was clear it would be our last World Cup. We all thought, 'We can't lose. This is our last chance.'

"I said before that in 1958 we had the best players but in 1970 we had the best team. We were very united. For me, it was the most important cup of my career. It was my best World Cup.

"When we arrived in Mexico we had a group mind-set ... of thinking, of prayer. We all thought we were going to win. We said it all the time.

"The game against England was probably our toughest game. In reality, our concern was not Italy. Italy was on very good form, but our worry was about the Germans because we thought that Germany could beat Italy in the semi-final and we'd have to face them in the final.

"When we got past England, which was very tough, and saw that Italy had beaten Germany, who we really didn't want to play, we were relieved. We knew how the Italians played. We were ready. We practised set pieces a lot. This worked, with example, Carlos Alberto's goal. Psychologically, we were a very strong union."

Tarcisio Burgnich, the Italian defender who marked Pelé in the 1970 final, said afterwards: "I told myself before the game, he's made of skin and bones just like everyone else – but I was wrong." *Pelé scored the first goal after 18 minutes from a perfect cross by Rivelino.*

"When people see my goal, they see the cross and they ask, 'How did you manage to jump so high?' [Giacinto] Facchetti and the others are 1 metre 90, 1 metre 80. I say, 'It was God's work. God took hold of me and lifted me up to score the goal.' It is one of the favourite goals of my career.

"We ended up conceding an early goal, which we weren't expecting, but it didn't shake us. We just carried on as if it hadn't happened.

"Even though we were winning, there was still great tension. All your thoughts are on the pitch. You think about the end of the game and victory but all your thoughts are on the game. It's as soon as the final whistle goes that you think about your family, your friends and all the people of Brazil.

"And then it's a big party."

↑ **Pelé opens the scoring for Brazil in the 18th minute.**

Pelé is regarded as the greatest footballer of all time. He remained at Santos throughout his career, retiring in 1974. He came out of retirement the following year to play for New York Cosmos. His final match was an exhibition between NY Cosmos and Santos in October 1977.

Pelé is the leading goal scorer for Brazil, with 77 goals in 91 matches, and is the only person to play in three World Cup-winning teams – in 1958, 1962 and 1970. England's 1966 captain, Bobby Moore, described him as "The most complete player I ever saw. He had everything." Sir Bobby Charlton from the same team said, "I sometimes feel as though football was invented for this magical player."

In 1999 Pelé was voted World Player of the Century by the International Federation of Football History & Statistics, and in the same year the International Olympic Committee voted him the Athlete of the Century. He has been a UNICEF ambassador since 1994 and has raised millions for children's charities including Great Ormond Street Hospital (London, UK) and Harlem Youth Soccer Association (New York City).

Roberto

BONINSEGNA

TEAM	**Italy**
BORN	**13 November 1943**
THE MATCH	**In 1970 the FIFA World Cup™ was hosted by Mexico. The final was played on 21 June in the Estadio Azteca, Mexico City.**
ATTENDANCE	**107,412**
RESULT	**Brazil 4-1 Italy**
THE GOAL	**Boninsegna scored the equaliser for Italy in the 37th minute.**
PHOTOGRAPHED	**on the main lake in Mantua, Lombardy**

I taly had had a disastrous World Cup in 1966. Arriving in England among the
favourites, they left disgraced after the first round, losing to North Korea, a team of
semi-professionals. The Azzurri were lambasted when they got home.

"So, I was in the initial 40. Being in the 40 I was obviously hoping to be called up
and to make it into the 22 to go to Mexico. But when the list came out I wasn't on it. I
wasn't there and I just thought, 'Oh well ...' I saw who had been called up – there were
three strikers. There was Luigi Riva, Pietro Anastasi and Bobo [Sergio] Gori. Then I
was told that Sandro Mazzola was to be the fourth striker.

I thought it was personal. Ferruccio Valcareggi, our coach, didn't like me.

"So when the call-up did come it was unexpected because I wasn't in the final 22. We were out fishing on the lake. We had a hut; it isn't there anymore unfortunately because the council knocked it down. My wife came running out. She was on this jetty, shouting that she'd received a telephone call from the Italian Federation and that I had to leave immediately for Mexico because Anastasi was injured, that I had to go to Milan to the consulate and get all the documents I needed.

"I said, 'Are you sure you understood them?' because it was very strange. It's not every day you go to a World Cup and also because by then I'd lost hope. Basically, I was already on holiday. She said, 'No, no, I understood fine. I spoke to someone from the Federation. I made him say it again. Here I've got the address of where you have to go to Milan.' So the connection between this lake and the World Cup is always there.

"When I got to the airport I saw Pierino Prati, the Milan striker. He was going to Mexico, too. I said, 'Gosh, now we're going to arrive in Mexico and there's going to be 23 of us.' This is what was ridiculous. When we got to the hotel the others are saying, 'What? There's two of you!' Now there was 23 of us, so someone had to go home because you were only allowed 22 players in the squad. So they sent home Giovanni Lodetti, who played for Milan too. Of course, he'd been in the original 22 so he didn't want to go home. You've got four years to prepare for the World Cup and then this happens.

"My biggest problem was the altitude. Mexico City is at 2,000 metres and it's very hard to breathe. The rest of the team had already been there and had acclimatised so I really struggled initially."

The Italians had a gruelling semi-final against West Germany. Roberto Boninsegna had put the Italians ahead after 8 minutes but [Karl-Heinz] Schnellinger snatched an equaliser in injury time. Italy won the match 4-3 but it left them drained ahead of the final, four days later.

"The night before the final a mariachi band came to play outside our hotel so we couldn't sleep. We couldn't sleep anyway. We played some cards and eventually got some sleep. I woke up more tired than I'd gone to bed. It was stressful.

↓ **Boninsegna (number 20) takes advantage of confusion in the Brazilian defence.**

"What an atmosphere at the stadium! The stadium was packed, obviously – it was a World Cup Final. There were over 100,000 spectators. Maybe 5,000 for us and 95,000 for Brazil. We arrived, the two buses, us and the Brazilians together, by chance. We were really serious, very focused. We could hear there was music on their bus. We were surprised but I suppose that makes sense. Brazilians love music. They did seem a bit more relaxed than us. though."

Brazil took the lead with a Pelé header after 18 minutes.

"I scored the goal because I knew that the Brazilians like playing around with the ball in their defense. They like holding on to the ball, showing off, doing their thing. I intercepted the ball that was passing across the field. When I saw this, I started closing down this player – I don't remember who it was – he tried to back heel it and I took the ball from him.

"Then I saw Brito coming in with a sliding tackle. I touched the ball and dribbled past him. Then I saw Félix come out and I moved left and there I came across Riva. We collided – I hadn't seen him there – and I took a strike. He lifted his legs, fortunately, because otherwise it would have been a rebound – basically, I had to dribble past Riva too!

"And then when I saw the ball go in ... the joy.

I've got a photo. It looks like I'm flying. And when I think about it again, I see the ball going in Brazil's goal!

"I equalised against Pelé's goal and it was the end of the first half. They had major players, not just Pelé. There was Rivelino, Jairzinho, Tostão. It was a great side. Gérson, too."

The score was still 1-1 at half-time.

"Maybe the extra time against West Germany cost us the final because we collapsed in the second half."

Gérson took the lead in the 66th minute. and from there the Brazilians turned on the flair. This was arguably the greatest World Cup team ever playing at their best. It was topped off by Carlos Alberto's goal in the 86th minute. It was a master class in team football and is considered to be the greatest World Cup Final ever.

"The defeat still burns, 4-1. We could have lost it differently, but it was a beautiful Brazil, a beautiful Brazil."

↑ **Boninsegna equalises for Italy in the 37th minute.**

Boninsegna was the top goal scorer for Inter Milan in the 1970-1 season. He stayed with the club until 1976, when he moved to bitter rivals, Juventus. He stayed there until 1979 when he went to Verona for a year before retiring. He lives in Mantua where he is technical director of his local team, Mantova FC.

MEXICO 70 ® TM FIFA

GÉRSON
de Oliveira Nunes

TEAM	**Brazil**
BORN	**11 January 1941**
THE MATCH	**In 1970 the FIFA World Cup™ was hosted by Mexico. The final was played on 21 June in the Estadio Azteca, Mexico City.**
ATTENDANCE	**107,412**
RESULT	**Brazil 4-1 Italy**
THE GOAL	**Gérson scored Brazil's second goal in the 66th minute.**
PHOTOGRAPHED	**on the beach near his home in Rio de Janeiro**

Gérson came from a footballing family, with both his father and uncle playing as professionals. He was already in the national team by 1962, but a serious knee injury kept him from going to the Chile FIFA World Cup™ Finals. He had played in the 1966 finals in England but neither he nor Brazil made an impression that year. The team assembled by the Brazil manager Mário Zagallo in 1970 is widely considered to be the greatest World Cup side of all time, and Gérson is considered to have been the brains behind that team.

"I've always kept my professional life and my personal life separate. There was my family and there was my professional life. I never brought things home. My wife never came to see me play. She never came to the stadium. They are always two distinct things. So I left [for the World cup training] just as I would normally. My family wished me well and I left.

"We were in a training camp for about two months. You'd get a few free hours to go home while in Brazil and then we were away for ten weeks for the World Cup.

"I tore my hamstring, a small pull, about a fortnight before the finals. I was in constant treatment. I played the first game against Czechoslovakia but we were 4-1 up so Zagallo took me off to help me recover, I didn't play again until the quarter-final.

"The quarter-final was against Peru. This was complicated for us because their manager was one of our footballing heroes, Didi [Waldyr Pereira]. He was one of Brazil's greatest ever midfielders. He'd put together a great team. It was a hard and complicated game, but we managed to get through, and get through well.

"The game against Uruguay in the semi-final was complicated, too, because of what had happened in 1950 [see pages 10-15]. People were scared it might happen all over again. So, by the time we reached the final, Italy was not going to stop us.

"We already knew the Italian team and they'd just come from a tough game against the Germans. We knew how they played – technically and tactically.

"The final, as incredible as it might seem, was much easier than the route there. Zagallo was so intelligent that other coaches would come and watch our side train to find out how we were going to play. Very intelligent as a player – very intelligent man. I played with him, and against him. He was a very intelligent manager.

"To find out if the Italians were really man-marking, as soon as we started Zagallo took Jairzinho off the right wing and put him on the left wing. He took Rivelino off the left wing and put him on the right wing. If their markers followed them, then we knew they really were man-marking. So he switched them again – Jairzinho onto the right wing and Rivelino onto the left wing.

He called to us: he pulled Rivelino a bit more into the midfield, he opened it up for Tostão over there, Pelé came over here, Jairzinho came over here and Carlos Alberto came through here, which then allowed him to score that fourth goal – precisely because of this move that we used to do, all practised, all set up specifically to beat the Italian defence.

"So for us this game was easier because we knew what they would do

but they didn't know what we would do.

There was not much to say on the day of the match because everything that had needed to be said had been said in training.

"The game was at midday which we knew would suit us better than it did the Europeans. It was hot. At 34 degrees [Celsius/93 degrees Fahrenheit] we'd have a party at the beach, but the Italians would suffer in the heat. We had a *pagode* [celebratory samba] session on the bus on the way to the stadium. A tambourine, samba drum, a shaker. We always did this. We'd have some fun. I mean, we were the band. After Mexico had gone out they supported us and that was good, too, along the way.

"When you step out on to the pitch, the nerves stop, because you have a thousand things to do. There's the adrenaline that goes up, and so each one of us has his own reaction, but you don't let that come out. That's your own thing. The nerves that you

↓ **Mazzola for Italy and Brito and Gerson for Brazil struggle over control of the ball.**

have inside – 'What will it be like? Will things go well?' – you keep that to yourself. We were winning 1-0. Pelé scored, but during some confusion between our defence and the midfield, Italy equalised and it was still like that at half-time.

"In the second half, like Zagallo told us, Jairzinho switched position again. He came off the right and went to the left. He received a ball and came on the diagonal. He brought his marker with him. He would pass me and leave me the ball, or he would pass with the ball and I would distract his marker.

"So what happened was he came with his marker. I came in for a dummy. I took the ball. He passed and took his marker with him. I laid the ball out and hit it into the net.

"The emotion is indescribable. Now the interesting thing is this, as incredible as it might seem, I prefer a thousand times over to make the pass, like I did for Jairzinho's goal, for Pelé goal, rather than to score the goal. You might think: isn't scoring the whole point? It is. But I preferred the assist, the perfect pass, because that is what I trained to do. I didn't train to score goals. I trained to make crosses and passes. That was my duty. I would discuss it with the forwards, Jairzinho, Tostão and Pelé, how I was going to put in the pass and where they would be, and they knew what I was going to do and they worked accordingly to make my job easier. I scored this goal – great.

But I was much more satisfied with the passes I made for them to score a goal – rather than my goal. That's the truth."

Gérson's goal in the 66th minute broke the spirit of the struggling Italians. From there on it was an exhibition of some of the greatest football ever seen. Jairzinho's messy goal was well deserved. He was the only player to score in every game in the finals and Carlos Alberto's late goal is widely considered to be the best FIFA World Cup™ goal ever scored.

"When the final whistle went it was chaos. The fans lifted up Pelé. They grabbed at Tostão's clothes. He just had his underpants on and they wanted those. They carried him to the dressing room. And in the dressing room there was great happiness. Three-time champions! It seemed the Cup was to remain indefinitely with Brazil.

"We changed and came out to receive the trophy. Carlos Alberto, our captain, went up and got the trophy. It was total euphoria. Brazil doesn't stop for the elections or for the President. But Brazil stops for football.

"There's no work, no classes, no school, there's nothing, for everyone. There's no traffic. Everyone stops. Wherever you are, you turn on the television. Brazil is the country of football. Full stop. Everything stops for football. This is how we are.

"Look at me. People say it is the greatest team ever. Before I was just a kid playing football on the beach."

↑ **Gerson takes the lead for Brazil after 66 minutes.**

Gérson spent his entire career in Brazil, playing his final days at Fluminense FC, the club he had supported as a child, before retiring in 1974. He lives in Rio de Janeiro.

1970

Jair Ventura Filho

JAIRZINHO

TEAM	**Brazil**
BORN	**25 December 1944**
THE MATCH	**In 1970 the FIFA World Cup™ was hosted by Mexico. The final was played on 21 June in the Estadio Azteca, Mexico City.**
ATTENDANCE	**107,412**
RESULT	**Brazil 4–1 Italy**
THE GOAL	**In the 71st minute Jairzinho scored Brazil's third goal.**
PHOTOGRAPHED	**in the Rio de Janeiro favela Manguinhos, known locally as the Gaza Strip**

Jairzinho lived his early career in the shadow of his idol, the bandy-legged genius Garrincha. He joined his local Rio team, Botafogo de Futebol e Regatas, rising up through the youth set-up while Garrincha was established in the first team. Jairzinho's preferred position was on the right wing, but that was Garrincha's position, so when he made his debut at 15 it was as centre forward. He made his international debut in 1964 when Garrincha was injured. It was not until Garrincha retired that Jairzinho took his place at both club and national level, on the right wing. He played in Brazil's unsuccessful 1966 FIFA World Cup™ campaign and was first choice on the right wing come 1970.

"When we won the first game against Czechoslovakia, we said, 'Just five left.' When we won against England, we said, 'Only four left.' And when we beat Uruguay we said, 'Just one left, people. Just one to go.'

"The right wingers were me and Rogério. In the first week at our training camp Rogério got injured, so that left just me. [Mário] Zagallo would often talk to the players individually. He took me aside and said, 'Jair, I have total confidence in you, and because of this I'm not going to call up another player to play on the wing. We're going to count on you.' I thanked him for putting his trust in me. It meant a lot.

"When Mexico went out, the whole of Mexico supported Brazil. Italy had put them out, so they especially wanted us to win. They all came out onto the streets. We struggled to get our bus into the stadium because of the fans lining the streets. I think the Italians felt quite intimidated with the huge number of fans supporting us.

"It had rained a fair bit the previous day so we were keen to see the state of the pitch. Normally, we played in moulded-rubber studs but because of the rain we played with longer aluminium studs. And then we went to warm up, as normal, each one encouraging the other:

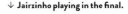

↓ **Jairzinho playing in the final.**

'It's today, it's today, it's today, it's today, it's today!'

"When we came out of the dressing room we stood alongside the Italians in the tunnel waiting to go up. We looked over at them but they wouldn't look at us. We were stamping our metal studs. It must have been quite intimidating because they looked very tense.

"Zagallo was very tactical. He thought of everything. He would draw out the pitch lines on a table and use bottle tops with numbers on them for the players. Today they have magnetic charts and you can add or remove players. This was how he'd work out his game plan and then he'd show us, giving each of us very specific instructions on the best way to play. It worked.

"They tested us in the opening minutes. Gigi Riva, their striker, forced Félix, our keeper, to make a couple of great saves. Pelé scored for us, but then Clodoaldo made a mistake at the back and lost the ball. Boninsegna got the ball and finished it, making it 1-1. It stayed like that until half-time.

"We came back for the second half with much more fight in us, more effectiveness. Gérson made it 2-1, which gave us more confidence.

"I scored what I considered the title-winning goal,

and it was 3-1 and they basically gave up.

"There was a move that I used to do a lot at Botafogo with Gérson. For me, after Didi, Gérson was the best passer of the ball I had ever seen. He could make a pass of more than 30 metres and it would land right at your feet.

"I took off on my run. Gérson was out on the left. He crossed into the penalty area. I called to Pelé and he headed it on. My first touch was to control the ball, and when I was about to finish it, Facchetti pushed me, knocking me off balance so that, as the ball went over the line, I followed it into the net. That's how I scored my goal.

"Then we finished with an amazing tactical goal that we had practised in training. Carlos Alberto scored it. The final goal of the tournament.

"When the referee blew the whistle,

an avalanche of Mexican fans invaded the pitch,

running all over us, cheering and grabbing at our clothes. When I left the pitch I was wearing only my pants! I saw photos afterwards – I still have them at home in magazines. The Mexicans lifted me up, not just me, all of the players, but mainly me.

"When I touched it, I think I'd never kissed anything with as much emotion as at the ceremony where I kissed the Cup.

"There were six of us in the national team from Botafogo. Brito was from Botafogo and went on loan to Flamengo. Gérson, Roberto Miranda, Paulo Cézar [Caju], Rogério and me. So, going back to the club was crazy. I couldn't go out on the streets. I was lucky I lived near the club so I could sneak in. People wanting to talk to you and wanting autographs. It lasted ... it basically lasted over 30 years."

↑ **Jairzinho scrambles the ball into the net in the 71st minute.**

Jairzinho became only the second player ever to have scored in every match while at the FIFA World Cup™ Finals (Uruguay's Alcides Ghiggia was the other). After the 1970 FIFA World Cup™ he went to play briefly for Olympique de Marseille. He also played for Portuguesa FC in Venezuela, before returning to Brazil. He retired from playing in 1982 and has had several managing jobs since with varying degrees of success.

Nicknamed the "Furacão da Copa" ("The Hurricane of the World Cup"), Jairzinho was voted number 27 in World Soccer magazine's 100 greatest players of the 20th century, one place above Zinedine Zidane (see page 193). He lives in Rio de Janeiro where he works with underprivileged kids in Rio's favelas.

MEXICO 70 © TM FIFA

CARLOS ALBERTO
Torres

TEAM	**Brazil**
BORN	**17 August 1944–25 October 2016**
THE MATCH	**In 1970 the FIFA World Cup™ was hosted by Mexico. The final was played on 21 June in the Estadio Azteca, Mexico City.**
ATTENDANCE	**107,412**
RESULT	**Brazil 4-1 Italy**
THE GOAL	**Carlos Alberto scored Brazil's fourth goal in the 86th minute.**
PHOTOGRAPHED	**at the Maracanã Stadium, Rio de Janeiro**

Brazil had failed to make any kind of impression on the 1966 FIFA World Cup™ and, despite winning in 1958 and 1962, had lost the confidence of the fans. Carlos Alberto, in spite of holding a regular place in the Brazil side, was dropped for the team a week before they left for England. Now, four years later, in 1970 Brazil had replaced their manager and Carlos Alberto was captain.

"I remember 1958. I was only 13 years old. I followed the World Cup, listening on the radio. I started dreaming about becoming a football player. My father and mother were radically against me becoming a football player. They used to say that football didn't put a shirt on your back. But, luckily, by the time I was 15 years old I was playing for Fluminense FC youth team. At 18 I was already a first-team player for Brazil.

"The Brazilians only want to win. We would see other countries being runners-up in the World Cup and still welcomed home like heros.

Here in Brazil, if you were runner-up, you wouldn't even come home.

There's no interest in second place.

"In the preparations for 1966 I was in the first team. I was 21 years old and in peak physical condition, but a week before the team was due to leave for England I was dropped. It was a complete shock. It was a real disappointment that no one at the time understood. It didn't make me feel any better that the team didn't do well and that journalists and fans said I was missed.

"Maybe it was because of 1966 but there was a real lack of faith from the fans before we travelled to Mexico. They didn't think we could raise our game.

"João Saldanha had been our coach. He didn't do so well and didn't get on with the players so they replaced him with Mário Zagallo. He was a very intelligent coach. He had been very successful at Botafogo and now he swapped this for the Brazil team. The players respected him and regarded his as their most experienced team-mate.

"Being captain of the team was something that happened naturally for me. Because in 1966 I was 22 years old. I was already the captain of Santos FC, which at the time was considered the best team in the world: Pelé, Coutinho, Pepe and Gilmar all played there.

"In one way we had an advantage dealing with the Brazilian fans because of the lack of information we had. Today, for example, a player phones home and they say, 'Oh, I just saw on the television, the commentator was criticising you.' Back then, only after three or four days could you get this information because of the difficulty in communications.

"It's not really until the first game that you really know what the capabilities of the team are, technically, physically and mentally. Our first match against Czechoslovakia was a bit up and down. They scored first but we won 4-1, so we knew we were in good shape.

"The second game was against England, the World Cup champions. We knew that, if we won, we'd get to the final. The English thought the same thing. Whoever won that match would be in the final. If we won, we would top our group and it would allow us to stay at Guadalajara, which is almost at sea level.

"And that's what happened. We had a great team. Not just Pelé, but Jairzinho, Tostão, Gérson, Rivelino, Clodoaldo and me – I let myself include me in this. Pelé was

↓ **Carlos Alberto celebrates scoring Brazil's fourth goal and Pelé runs to congratulate him.**

↑ **Carlos Alberto celebrates scoring arguably the greatest World Cup Final goal ever.**

Gérson was on tambourine, Jairzinho played the drum. All of us took part. We got to the stadium, we went to the changing room, had a little coffee. Some players had a rest; some even had a nap. Then we went out onto the pitch and saw the stadium. You feel the energy of the fans. The majority of the Mexican fans were on our side. That helped. It's a series of small details that helps you win a game.

"The first 15 minutes were tense – for both teams, I think. Slowly, we began to find our feet and then Pelé scored, which calmed us a lot. Even after Clodoaldo's mistake and their goal, we stayed calm. Pelé scored a second goal, but the referee decided to blow the whistle for the end of the first half before Pelé put the ball in.

"We knew it was a matter of patience. Not long into the second half Gérson gave us the goal we needed.

"After Jairzinho's goal (the third) we were just waiting for the time to pass so we could celebrate. There's one detail that not many people know about the goal I scored. People think it happened just like that – I got there, Pelé passed it to me – but, no, there was more to it than that.

"Zagallo had told us, if when they were attacking us, you saw Tostão, Jairzinho and Pelé move to the left, that right-hand side of our attack would be wide open, completely free for a possible entry by me. It was only a question of being switched on and ready. And we were, because the whole game was being played over on the left with Clodoaldo, Piazza, Gérson, Rivelino. Then the ball went to Jairzinho. When the ball went to Jairzinho, I set off. I remembered what Zagallo had said. When the ball came quickly to Pelé, he just glanced to his side and saw that I was coming, because he was switched on too, about what Zagallo had said. He rolled the ball to his right and I scored the goal.

"So that was me, scoring a goal in the final, a few minutes before the end of the game. Soon after I was standing there as captain, lifting the Jules Rimet Trophy, representing my country and my team-mates.

A lot of things go through your head – family, friends, the fans – it's indescribable.

I was 25, the youngest captain in all World Cup history. Even now, no one calls me Carlos Alberto; they call me *O Capitão* – 'The Captain'."

a great example of humility – a team player. He was already the king of football, but, because he was such a humble guy and thought only of the team, no one else could allow themselves not to be like that too.

"The semi-final was against Uruguay, which 20 years earlier had been the cause of Brazil's greatest failure here in the Maracanã, in the 1950 World Cup Final. The fans were very worried. I don't remember that game because I was too young. The Brazilians, even at the door of our hotel, were saying, 'Gosh, do you think it will be a repeat of what happened in '50?' It had a negative effect on the players. In the game, Brazil broke the taboo of this thing we always have with Uruguay. Brazil won well.

"Because of the time difference the games would be played at midday. On the day of the final we were woken at 7am to have lunch. It was a pre-match meal that they called "food", but which consisted of super-strength coffee and nothing else. We would eat after the match.

"When we left the hotel to go to the stadium, we had our traditional Brazilian dance percussion group in the bus. We were the band.

After the FIFA World Cup™, Carlos Alberto returned to Santos FC, where he stayed until 1974 when he went back to his first club, Fluminense FC. In 1977 he went to play for New York Cosmos alongside Pelé and Franz Beckenbauer. He retired from playing in 1982 and had many managerial posts including at Fluminense FC, Miami Sharks (United States) and, on the international scene, Oman and, latterly, Azerbaijan, where he finished his managerial career in 2005. As a player, manager and subsequently a pundit he was known for his no-nonsense attitude. He will always be remembered for his goal in the 1970 final, considered to be the greatest FIFA World Cup™ goal ever scored. He died after a heart attack on 25 October 2016.

Johan NEESKENS

TEAM	**Netherlands**
BORN	**15 September 1951**
THE MATCH	**In 1974 the FIFA World Cup™ Final was hosted by West Germany. The final was played on 7 July in the Olympiastadion, Munich.**
ATTENDANCE	**78,200**
RESULT	**West Germany 2-1 Netherlands**
THE GOAL	**Neeskens scored a penalty in 2nd minute.**
PHOTOGRAPHED	**by the Black Sea, Istanbul**

The Total Football playing style, refined by manager Marinus "Rinus" Michels at Amsterdam team AFC Ajax, dominated European football throughout the 1970s. It allowed players to move around the pitch as they saw fit and to cover for those who had left what was their designated position. Michels spotted 19-year-old Neeskens in 1970 and soon had him playing an integral role within the team. They won the European Cup in the 1971-2, 1972-3 and 1973-4 seasons. That Total Football style was carried over into the Dutch national team, making the Netherlands the most exciting and, arguably, the best team in the world come the finals in 1974.

"I was playing for a couple of years for my local team in the second division, in the Netherlands, and scouts used to come and see us, from Feyenoord, FC Twente and Ajax. We went to play an under-18 tournament in Scotland and met East Germany in the final. It was a tie and then extra time. There were no penalties then, so the referee had a piece of wood, on one side red and on the other side blue. He tossed it up and we lost. It was very disappointing but a scout from Ajax was there and he called me. They were my favourite team. I was a fan. They played beautiful football. I thought it might take a year and a half to make the first team, but I played with them from the start and got a call-up for the national team the same year, aged just 19.

"It was Mr Michels at Ajax Amsterdam who created what we now call Total Football. It meant you played your position but anyone could attack, and if they were up front, someone else would cover whatever their position was. So defenders could attack and strikers would cover for them. It worked. We won the European Cup three times in a row. For a country as small as the Netherlands that's amazing. There were seven players from that Ajax team in the national team in 1974. We played the same way as we did at Ajax.

"We always had music on the bus, and pretty loud music, too. We would be singing very loudly until we arrived at the stadium. Going to the stadium there was already a lot of Germans though not so many Dutch people.

"In the tunnel, of course, you look at each other, but

we weren't afraid of the Germans at all, not at all.

"We started to play. The Germans hadn't touched the ball and I'd had only two touches and all of a sudden we got a penalty. It was a little strange because it's the final, and after only two minutes you're not feeling so good. You've hardly touched the ball. You're not warmed up, and the whole world is watching.

"I placed the ball and turned my back, which I always did. While I was running up, I was thinking which side I was going to shoot, and that was a mistake because I changed my mind. By the last step I was thinking, 'No, I'm going to shoot the other way', but in my stride I didn't plan out how to do that so I ended up hitting it very hard down the middle. Sepp Maier [the German goalkeeper] had watched my penalty kicks. He went to the side that I had scored against Bulgaria, but luckily he went too early. The whole world was watching so I can understand there were some nerves, but I always say, 'Don't change your mind.' But I did it myself. I'm only human.

"It was a great feeling to see the ball in the net. I thought, 'We're going to win it.'

"Maybe it was too early. Normally, when we scored we'd go for a second, but all of a sudden I don't know why, there was no sign of that.

It was not that the coach said, 'Hey, now keep possession' – it just happened and Cruyff was just playing the ball easy, playing it back and forth. I'm more a player who tries to steal the ball and go up front and try to hurt the opponents, but we didn't do that and I think that was a big mistake. We let them back in the game.

"Now when you speak to people about that final they say, 'It's a pity you guys didn't win. You deserved to win that one because of the way you played.' On the other hand, you can play the most beautiful football, but it doesn't guarantee you're going to win and that's what happened to us.

"It was only a final!"

↑ **Neesken's scores his penalty to take the lead for Holland after only 2 minutes.**

Rinus Michels and team-mate Johan Cruyff left Ajax for FC Barcelona in 1973. After the FIFA World Cup™, Neeskens followed them to Spain. He stayed there until 1979 when, like so many of his peers, he went to play in the United States, for New York Cosmos during the North American Soccer League's heyday.

Neeskens retired from playing in 1991 and has managed numerous clubs since.

1974

Paul
BREITNER

TEAM	**West Germany**
BORN	**5 September 1951**
THE MATCH	**In 1974 the FIFA World Cup™ was hosted by West Germany. The final was played on 7 July in the Olympiastadion, Munich.**
ATTENDANCE	**78,200**
RESULT	**West Germany 2-1 Netherlands**
THE GOAL	**In the 25th minute Breitner scored the equaliser from the penalty spot.**
PHOTOGRAPHED	**at the Olympiastadion, Munich**

Although West Germany were technically at home, hosting the FIFA World Cup™, the Netherlands were favourites. The Dutch team consisted largely of the Total Football–playing Ajax team who were the best in Europe. Breitner, nicknamed "der Afro" because of his hair, scored the only goal in their opening match against Chile.

"When I was six years old I was playing with 14-year-olds. That's not because they thought I was a nice chap but because I was able to play with boys much older. In 1970 I signed for FC Bayern Munich. I signed a professional contract to get the money for my studies but by the end of the first year I was playing for the national side and my mind was made up."

West Germany were slow to start, only coming second in their group after losing to neighbouring East Germany.

"The semi-final against Poland wasn't fun. The Polish were, in my opinion, the best team in that World Cup. Not the Dutch. Not us. The match was delayed by 45 minutes because the pitch was waterlogged. The fire brigade came to pump out the water so it was only just playable. I say 'only just', but it is as obvious today as it was back then, that the pitch actually wasn't playable. But because of the scheduling the match had to go ahead.

"We beat the Polish 1-0 in that water battle, because the Polish didn't understand how they were supposed to play on that surface. They played with real finesse, but that was never going to work.

↓ **Breitner shoots from the penalty spot in the 25th minute.**

We played a more primitive football.

You have to make sure that the ball goes as far and as fast as possible upfield, no matter how. It's not technically perfect but it worked. By the time the Polish realised this, we were 1-0 up and they never got back into it.

"And then the final here in Munich against the Netherlands.

"The day itself, as regards preparation, was just like before any other match. Everyone could have breakfast whenever they liked, and at 11 o'clock we had our meeting. It was a journey of maybe 20 minutes.

"When we were in the stadium something happened that gave us that last burst of motivation. It had a sort of turbo impact on us. When we arrived in the changing room and went out to view the pitch and then went back in, the Dutch started, in the changing room opposite ours, to celebrate, to chant, to jeer like a bunch of guys at the Oktoberfest [Munich's annual beer festival]. We were sitting in the changing room looking at each other thinking: 'What are they doing? Are they taking the piss? Are they making fun of us?' This caused a lot of anger and gave us the last bit of uncompromising will to fight and give it everything.

"We went out, the referee blew the whistle and, without any of us – or hardly any of us – having seen what was going on, we were behind 1-0.

"The Dutch weren't able to deal with the 1-0 lead. They didn't take advantage of the minutes that followed. They didn't sense that we were totally down. You go into the World Cup Final and after one minute you are behind 1-0. You just want to go home.

"Just as we had suspected in the changing room, they were celebrating in advance. They wanted to make fun of us. They made us run, they outplayed us, but they absolutely weren't keen on scoring a second goal.

"After about 25 minutes we got a penalty.

"We hadn't determined a penalty taker, and I was the last one they would have chosen, or the second last one, but I knew that no one wanted to assume the responsibility. Something was building up in me, so I said to myself, 'OK, boy, you want to be World Cup champion? Taking this penalty is part of it, so you will do this now. You put it away and that's that.'

"I went to the penalty spot, I placed the ball, I went back to the 18-yard line and then Wolfgang Overath came up to me (he told me that afterwards, because I don't remember it).

↑ **Breitner equalises for West Germany in the 25th minute.**

Two minutes of the final are missing in my memory.

There was a cut, a mind-blank. And he said to me: 'Paul, what's going on? Do you want to take the penalty?' I said: 'What do you think I am doing here, Wolfgang? I am going to put it away ... Now sod off!' ... And then it was in the net.

"The final was on a Sunday. On Monday morning at about 8, 8.30am, I came home from the celebrations with my wife, and I switched on the TV. I told myself: 'You just lie down on the sofa and with one eye you just watch this beautiful final again, just to sober up.'

"I see Bernd Hölzenbein falling and I see referee Taylor pointing to the penalty spot and then I see the number 3 – that was me – walking out of the picture. Five seconds later the number 3 comes back and walks towards the penalty spot. I jumped to my feet. I felt sick and started sweating, I was dripping with sweat, sweat running down my forehead, I was finished. I went to the TV and switched it off. I was thinking, 'Are you crazy? What are you doing!? What happens if you can't put it away?' I went to my wife and said, 'I have to go out – I can't bear it. I am going for a walk.' I went for a walk for half an hour and started to think: 'What did you do? Why did you do that?'

"I am telling you that because two minutes of this final are missing in my memory.

"I don't remember seeing Gerd Müller's goal. I only remember the seemingly endless cheering of the crowds, but not how the goal happened. I was on the other side of the pitch. I do remember thinking, 'We made it. We made it!'

"And then the final whistle.

"I could tell you how I felt in the first minutes after that, but it wouldn't be of any use. No one would be able to relate to it."

Breitner won the European Cup in the same year, meaning he had won everything there was to win by the age of 22. In search of new challenges, he went to Real Madrid CF for three years where he won two league championships and the Spanish Cup title.
He returned to FC Bayern Munich and also scored again in the FIFA World Cup™ Final in 1982 where West Germany lost to Italy (see page 139).

1974

© TM FIFA

Gerd MÜLLER

TEAM	**West Germany**
BORN	**3 November 1945**
THE MATCH	**In 1974 the FIFA World Cup™ was hosted by West Germany. The final was played on 7 July in the Olympiastadion, Munich.**
ATTENDANCE	**78,200**
RESULT	**West Germany 2-1 Netherlands**
THE GOAL	**In the 43rd minute Müller scored the winning goal.**
PHOTOGRAPHED	**at FC Bayern Munich grounds**

Müller, at just 1.75m (5ft 9in), seemed too short to be a footballer, let alone a striker. Nicknamed "Der Bomber", he was a prolific goal scorer, notable for his ability to poach goals in the six-yard box. He made his debut for West Germany aged 18 in 1966 and quickly established himself in the first team. At the 1970 FIFA World Cup™ Finals he had scored ten goals in six matches, earning him the Golden Boot in spite of his team not making it to the final.

"I joined Bayern when I was 17. There is no better club for mentoring young players. I had offers from Barcelona but I decided to stay here at Bayern. No one ever regrets coming here. I've been the top scorer here six times.

"We lost to the GDR [East Germany] and then there was a row in the camp among the players. There were arguments about how we should be playing.

We weren't playing well. I don't think we played that well throughout the tournament.

Schön [Helmut Schön, Germany manager 1964-78] was banging his fists on the table. He was furious, but after everyone had said their piece things were much better.

"The day before the final I read in a newspaper that a fortune-teller had looked into her crystal ball and predicted that the Netherlands would win. I'm not superstitious but I almost couldn't sleep because I kept on thinking of the Dutch and of the fortune-teller and I thought, 'This can't be true.' And the Dutch maybe even believed that she was right, but we said to ourselves that we would put a stop to the fortune-teller's game.

"We were a little scared of the Netherlands and we immediately conceded a penalty. But I have to say that the Dutch were pretty stuck up and thought that they had the Germans in the bag. Yes, I thought it was over ... I didn't believe. It was more likely that we would lose against them than that they would win against us. But a German team isn't so easy to bring down. We said to ourselves: 'Now we will fight more than ever. Now we will give it our all.'

"Bonhof and Grabowski came from the right and that was where the goal was, where I was. I was going forward, then back again. I was lucky. Three Dutchmen were all going forward when the ball went to my left foot and I kicked the ball into the far corner [of the goal].

"And you keep on looking at the clock – to see how much time is left.

And the time doesn't go by, the time doesn't go by, and you keep on looking over. And when the final whistle came, we cheered. When I played for the national team I scored 68 goals in 62 internationals. I scored many important goals, many of them in cup finals – there are so many – but the World Cup is the most important.

"The celebration dinner that night was badly organised. Our wives weren't allowed in. They were downstairs having more fun than us. That wasn't FIFA's fault, it was our own fault, the German Football Federation's. But then we all went to a club together. I can't remember the name of it."

↑ **Müller turns to score the winner for West Germany in the 43rd minute.**

Müller retired from international football after the 1974 final, having scored a staggering 68 goals in 62 appearances. He stayed at FC Bayern Munich until 1979 when he joined Fort Lauderdale Strikers in the United States. At Bayern, he scored 365 goals in 427 games. After three seasons in America he retired from playing. In subsequent years he fell into chronic alcoholism. His old club rallied round and played an integral part in his full recovery, giving him a job as youth coach. Today he continues to live in Munich.

Mario
KEMPES

TEAM	**Argentina**
BORN	**15th July 1954**
THE MATCH	**In 1978 the FIFA World Cup™ was hosted by Argentina. The final was played on 25 June in the Estadio Antonio Vespucio Liberti ("El Monumental"), Buenos Aires.**
ATTENDANCE	**71,483**
RESULT	**Argentina 3-1 Netherlands**
THE GOAL	**Kempes scored in the 37th minute and the 14th minute of extra time.**
PHOTOGRAPHED	**at home in Buenos Aires**

The 1978 FIFA World Cup™ remains shrouded in rumour and controversy. The host nation, Argentina, was ruled by a brutal military junta, which has been accused of interfering with the tournament for its own ends. The rumours were further fuelled when Argentina needed to win their semi-final against neighbours Peru by four clear goals. They won 6-0, a score sheet unheard of at the finals.

Kempes was the only player playing outside Argentina at the time of selection. Playing for Valencia CF, he had been the top scorer in La Liga (the Spanish Premier Division) for the previous two seasons.

"I was born in Bell Ville in the province of Córdoba. My old man was an accountant at a carpentry workshop and mum did the housework. My dad always supported me in wanting to play football. Every dad wants his son to play football. At school breaks we'd play with wooden plugs or scrunched-up balls of paper. Anything we could find really. I've played since as long as I can remember. My earliest memory is carrying a ball under my arm.

"I was playing in Spain, and never thought that the national team would call me again, but in '78 I was lucky that [César] Menotti called me. The national team never crossed my mind: because I was so far away, it wasn't normal [to be called up]. All the others played in Argentina."

Argentina's failure to win their group meant that they had to leave the capital, Buenos Aires, for Rosario, where Kempes had played until 1976. The format of the competition meant that there were two group stages rather than a knockout stage to get to the final. This was why in their final group match Argentina needed to win by four clear goals.

"The morning of the final was like any other. You're nervous before the first match. César's [Menotti] team talk was the shortest of the tournament. Basically, everything had been talked about.

"On the way to every game, as soon as we left the camp, on the coach, there was always a lady standing on the first corner holding a Virgin Mary, but she wasn't there on the day of the final. Maybe we just couldn't see her because of the crowds.

"It's a spectacular thing going out onto the pitch from the changing rooms: you go down the stairs, then walk straight and then you go up again. When the team comes out they start throwing ticker tape. It's like when the Christians went out into the arena in Rome, in the Colosseum. I don't know if the Dutch got stage fright or not, but we were used to it.

"The first goal came from a play on the left side, started by [Osvaldo] Ardiles. He passed it to [Leopoldo] Luque, who punted it down the middle, and

I saw the chance.

I threw myself [towards the ball]; Jongbloed, the goalie, was coming out and the ball passed right below his stomach.

"You know you are winning 1-0, but you forget, because you are playing, that at any moment they could score a goal against you. And Nanninga's header did make it 1-1.

"The referee Sergio Gonella blew the final whistle, and then another game started. Well, the second goal was quite similar to the first, because of a foul, and a play with Bertoni, Ardiles, Luque. Two Dutch players were coming out. I don't know if I was closer to the ball, or they were slow, or I was faster, I'll never know. But I stretched my leg, and somehow I tapped the ball and,

by the time they reached it, it was already bouncing in.

"I celebrated behind the goal, and I don't know if anybody came to hug me, because the truth is everyone wanted to celebrate the goal their own way. At last we had made it. After all the work we had done, the prize had come to us, the prize for a team that had fought, that had sweated, that had trusted one another.

"And with all the calmness of the world we showered, and we knew we had to attend the awards dinner in some hotel. People were coming in, shouting 'Champions, champions!' but we were as if on another planet, you know?

"That night we got dressed up in our suits and went to the party. Somewhere around 7.30 or 8.00pm we went to the hotel, had dinner, and the prizes were awarded. At around 1 or 1.30 am I left with Loco [Daniel] Killer and [Américo] Gallego, who were from Rosario too. Loco had his car at the hotel, so he drove us, with the trophies, our bags and all, and we drove to Rosario, the three of us. We arrived around 7, 7.30am.

"He dropped me off at my house, I took my bags, my trophies, I took everything that I had, and there was nobody on the streets. With all the peace in the world I went to my front door, rang the bell, my mother asked who it was, I answered 'Me' and went up in the elevator with my prizes ... Nobody saw me. It was very quiet. No one was around.

"I wanted to go to Bell Ville, my home town, straight away but my dad said he needed to get the car fixed and it wouldn't be ready to go until noon. We eventually left at 5pm. As we got close to Bell Ville there were people on the streets with flags cheering. It was crazy. They took me and put me on top of a fire truck and drove me into town. It took over two hours to do the last six kilometres.

"It was euphoric but it was too crazy. I couldn't sleep, I couldn't even take a nap, so I went to Córdoba and went fishing with my friends, but word got out that I was there too, so I left and went back to Spain.

↑ **Kempes scores his second goal to give Argentina a lead.**

Kempes's two goals in the 1978 FIFA World Cup™ took his tally for that year's finals to six, winning him the Golden Boot for the highest goal scorer in the tournament. He also won the Golden Ball for Player of the Tournament. After the FIFA World Cup™ he returned to CF Valencia in Spain, where he remained until 1981, afterwards returning to Buenos Aires to play for CA River Plate. His stay only lasted a year before he went back to Valencia. He went on to manage numerous clubs in Albania, Venezuela, Bolivia and Indonesia.

Kempes is an ambassador for his old club CF Valencia and is an analyst and commentator with US sports channel ESPN. He lives in Connecticut.

1978

Dick
NANNINGA

TEAM Netherlands

BORN 17 January 1949–21 July 2015

THE MATCH In 1978 the FIFA World Cup was hosted by Argentina. The final was played on 25 June in the Estadio Antonio Vespucio Liberti (El Monumental), Buenos Aires.

ATTENDANCE 71,483

RESULT Argentina 3–1 Netherlands

THE GOAL In the 82nd minute Nanninga scored the equaliser.

PHOTOGRAPHER Romano Marie, KBK team

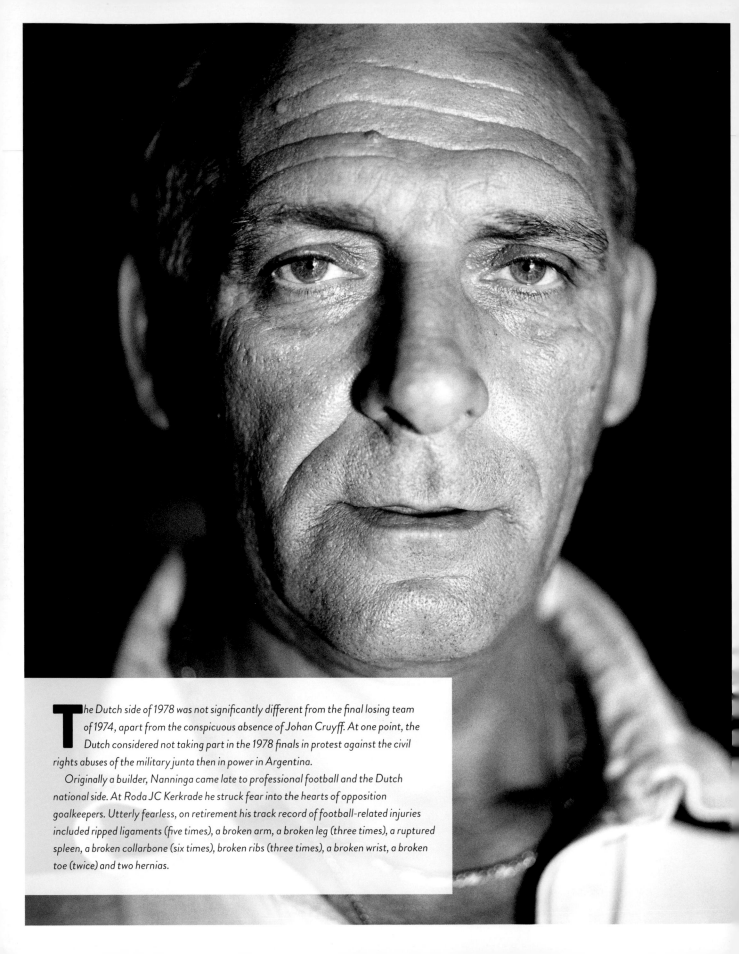

The Dutch side of 1978 was not significantly different from the final losing team of 1974, apart from the conspicuous absence of Johan Cruyff. At one point, the Dutch considered not taking part in the 1978 finals in protest against the civil rights abuses of the military junta then in power in Argentina.

Originally a builder, Nanninga came late to professional football and the Dutch national side. At Roda JC Kerkrade he struck fear into the hearts of opposition goalkeepers. Utterly fearless, on retirement his track record of football-related injuries included ripped ligaments (five times), a broken arm, a broken leg (three times), a ruptured spleen, a broken collarbone (six times), broken ribs (three times), a broken wrist, a broken toe (twice) and two hernias.

"I turned professional when I was 23 years old. Before that I worked in construction and before that as a machine fitter. When I became a professional footballer I started my own business, a flower shop. Now I work at Sphinx. It's the best sanitary-ware producer in the Netherlands. I have been working there for almost 25 years now. I love my job and football is in the past for me. I'm a family man. My children aren't really proud that I scored that goal, but the grandchildren are.

"Actually, I don't think about that goal anymore. It's 30 years ago. I am a real family man. I have three kids and six grandchildren. In fact, last Sunday my seventh grandchild was born.

"When I watched the World Cup Finals of 1974, I was still an amateur. Four years later I was playing in the final, in Argentina. It all happened so quickly. My first international match was one of the warm-up matches for the World Cup against Tunisia and I scored twice.

"Happel [Ernst Happel, Netherlands manager 1997-8] was a good tactical trainer but was not very good with people. I have actually never spoken to him longer than half a minute. He never said anything to me.

"At first we were in a hotel in the Andes. The world practically ended there. There were only mountains, nothing else. The training pitch would be frozen every morning.

↓ **Nanninga out jumps the Argentine defence to equalise in the 82nd minute.**

"When we went shopping we had police with us who were wearing the same tracksuits as us, but they also carried guns. They pretended to be part of our entourage. We could see guys with rifles on rooftops. It was all a bit strange. We didn't have any friends or family with us there.

"Johnny Rep was our preferred striker, and when that didn't work I would come on as a wild-card substitute. I was mentally prepared for that. At least I got on. There were some guys who went the whole way there and just sat on the bench. And they were good players.

"In the West Germany match I got sent off. Bernd Hölzenbein and me were pushing each other in the wall and we both got a yellow card. But as the ref was walking away someone else said, 'Stupid ref!' and the ref thought it was me and he sent me off. I'd only been on the pitch for seven minutes. Because of that I was suspended for the Italy match and then it was the final.

"Even the World Cup Final is just a football match.

The atmosphere was tense, of course, but not nervy. At the final there were only 500 Dutch people and 80,000 [sic] Argentines. The atmosphere at the stadium was crazy. I'd never seen anything like it. None of us had.

"The Dutch team already had a contract with Adidas and I had my own contract with Puma. They knew that at the Dutch team so they just brought shirts with two stripes for me.

"At half-time it was 1-0. You're eating yourself up on the bench, you want to get on and get the equaliser. I heard [Jan] Zwartkruis, our assistant coach. say at half-time, 'Now is the time to bring Dick on.' All Happel said to me was 'Warm up' in German, and I was on.

↑ **The Dutch celebrate Nanninga's late equaliser.**

"The goal came from the left from [Jan] Poortvliet to Arie Haan, and Arie Haan passed it to the midfielder. He played it to the right to [René] van der Kerkhof and I was in the centre and when the ball came

I knew it was going to be a goal. I could just feel it.

The pass was perfect.

"You want to win the match – 1-1 wasn't enough. Then, in the closing seconds, [Rob] Rensenbrink nearly did. He hit the post.

"In extra time they made it 2-1, and then 3-1, and it was done – you know you can't do anything anymore to win. The final whistle blew and we went in. We had lost. We went back into the changing room and the first thing I did was roll a cigarette and light it up. The mood was low. We had a few drinks that night, though.

"We had decided beforehand that, because of what was happening with the government in Argentina, if we won we wouldn't go and collect the cup, so they sent the medals to the hotel.

"We flew back the next day and I went back to work in the flower shop the day after. The neighbours had decorated the shop because we had got second place but I just went back to work.

"I was a labourer's son ... I still am. My greatest achievement is my kids and my grandchildren. I mean ... OK, it was in a World Cup Final, but it's still just a goal."

The Netherlands remain the greatest team to have never won the FIFA World Cup™.
Nanninga stayed at FC Roda for eight years, at one point turning down a move to AFC Ajax
as it would have meant leaving or selling the flower shop. After a brief spell in Hong Kong he
retired in 1986. In 2014 during an operation on his leg he went into a coma that lasted four
months. He died in the local hospital in Maaseik in northern Belgium on 21 July 2015.

1978

Daniel
BERTONI

TEAM	**Argentina**
BORN	**14 March 1955**
THE MATCH	**In 1978 the FIFA World Cup™ was hosted by Argentina. The final was played on 25 June in the Estadio Antonio Vespucio Liberti ("El Monumental"), Buenos Aires.**
ATTENDANCE	**71,483**
RESULT	**Argentina 3-1 Netherlands**
THE GOAL	**In the 25th minute of extra time Bertoni scored Argentina's third goal.**
PHOTOGRAPHED	**at home in Buenos Aires**

Argentina had been governed by a military junta since the coup d'etat which deposed Isabel Martínez de Perón in 1976. At one point the Dutch team considered boycotting the tournament in protest against the regime.

By 1987 Bertoni was already an established in the first team at CA Independiente just outside Buenos Aires and had been playing at national level since 1974.

"We had a really tough group. We couldn't guarantee beating any of them.

"I had picked up an injury before the tournament and wasn't certain of my place in the team. In the first match, against Hungary, I came on as a sub and scored the winner. I didn't play the second match (against France) but then I started against Italy. We lost. I didn't think I'd had a great game but Menotti [César Menotti, Argentina manager 1974-82] kept me in and I played in the rest of the games.

"The Netherlands was a complete team and we knew that we were up against one of the hardest rivals to beat. It was 'The Clockwork Orange' team – the team that played Total Football. Except for Cruyff´s absence, it was almost the same team as 1974. I think we knew what was at stake and where we were going.

"I remember when we left to go to the stadium … the streets were full of people. Every time we passed by there was an old lady, but on the day we played against Italy she wasn't there, she was with the Sacred Heart waiting for the national team. When we passed and did not see her, we all looked at each other, and then we lost. And then, she was there again on the day of the final. She had a figurine of Christ in her hand; it wasn't cabala, she was encouraging us, you know? When one is a believer you feel it that way. I believe it also gave us strength on the pitch.

"It meant everything, because we were playing a final. It wasn't just another game, and we wouldn't have another chance. We knew that we were up against [Rund] Krol, [René] van de Kerkhof; there was [Rob]Rensenbrink and [Johnny] Rep. They were great players.

"I lost count of how many times I went for a pee in the changing rooms. This wasn't any game. We'd never have another chance. We were prepared mentally. Menotti, Pizzarotti [the fitness trainer], the entire coaching team did a great job psychologically.

"It was all or nothing. It was a war. One of those finals you play to the death. Well, the walk through the tunnel … it was like when a boxer is walked to the ring. Us against them … no greetings, no handshakes, nothing. We said, 'It's us and the Dutch, 11 against 11.'

"When we went out onto the pitch we looked up and couldn't see anything really, the sky was covered by ticker tape.

↓ **Bertoni takes on the Dutch defence.**

The crowd really had a lot to do with our success.

"Then the match started a little later because [Daniel] Passarella saw one of the van der Kerkhof brothers with a bandaged hand and started arguing about whether he should be allowed to play. It was to make the Dutch nervous, to unsettle them. They were a great team – we couldn't make them nervous not even with that bandaged hand issue.

"We were winning 1-0 at half-time. Then in the second half they started to play better than us and then Nanninga scored. Just for a moment there was silence just as if everyone in the stadium had died.

"The crowd was important. They were really another player for us.

"I had started the match with bandages on my toes, shinpads, socks up all the way. At the end of 90 minutes my socks were down around my ankles, my shinpads were hanging off. Rensenbrink hit the post for them at full time. That was like a bucket of iced water being thrown over you.

"And then it was extra time.

↑ **Bertoni scores Argentina's third goal in the 115th minute.**

"When you start getting tired, your mind gets a little hazy, and on top of that, after a few minutes of the start of extra time, [Wim] Suurbier hit me on the top of my knee and I thought he had broken it. The doctor came and said, 'Get up, get up! There's nothing wrong with you.' I created the play for Kempes's second goal, and we were 2-1 up.

"We started passing the ball between each other in their box. The Dutch were very good at defending. Just in front of goal I was about to fall over and grabbed Kempes's shoulder and knocked him down. I was looking straight ahead at the goal, with the ball at my feet.

The goalkeeper made a wrong move and I scored the goal.

I always tell Mario [Kempes] that I didn't want him to score three goals on his own, so I stole his third goal.

"It is indescribable to talk about scoring a goal in a final. It's the greatest feeling. I remember that my mother and my wife told me that my father had left the stadium and hugged a small tree and just started crying.

"We gave the people great joy, at a time when a lot of people were experiencing a lot of pain due to the disappearance of a son, of a family member. All of that wasn't our fault. We were trying to make people happy. We played football, which was what we were trying to do the best we could.

"I never thought I was someone special."

After the World Cup Bertoni moved to Spain to play for Sevilla FC and then Italy where he played for Fiorentina, Napoli, Udinese and Avelino before retiring from playing in 1988. He had a brief spell as the coach of CA Independiente in 2004. He lives in Buenos Aires.

Paolo
ROSSI

TEAM	**Italy**
BORN	**23 September 1956**
THE MATCH	**In 1982 the FIFA World Cup™ was hosted by Spain. The final was played on 11 July in the Estadio Santiago Bernabéu, Madrid.**
ATTENDANCE	**90,000**
RESULT	**Italy 3-1 West Germany**
THE GOAL	**Rossi scored Italy's first goal in the 57th minute.**
PHOTOGRAPHED	**at his vineyard in Tuscany**

Prior to the 1982 FIFA World Cup™ Finals Rossi's career and reputation were in
tatters. At the height of his career, while playing at AC Perugia in 1980, he got
embroiled in a match-fixing scandal and was suspended from professional football
for three years. On appeal, this was reduced to two years. The Italians had a strong team
that made the semi-finals in 1978 but Rossi had not played for two years.

"It was during the 1970 World Cup – I was 14 – that I began to understand just
how important football is for Italy. You think, 'Will I ever make it myself?' and of
course it's very hard but there's a part of you that thinks 'Maybe, yes.'

"My dad really loved football, too. I have a clear memory of Santos [FC] coming to play in Florence when I was 12. Pelé was playing. My dad took me on the back of his Vespa. During the 1982 finals my father didn't come to Spain. He watched all the games at home.

"It was as though that whole affair, the scandal, in which I had been involved was now part of another world – it had had nothing to do with me, I just wanted to put it all behind me. So when it came to an end and my two-year suspension finished it was as though I was starting afresh with a new life.

"Obviously, I hadn't been back playing long. Most people didn't think I could get back into physical or mental form. I was only 26 years old.

↓ **Rossi scores Italy's first goal in the 57th minute.**

I wanted to show that I was still a major player, that I could do great things.

"Enzo Bearzot was a key person for me, not so much because he was the national coach but because I sensed the trust he had in me.

"In the first few games I found it really difficult to get back in the game mentally. I still wasn't ready. Everything was difficult. It was hard even to do easy things. At the end of the first half against Peru, when I got substituted, I felt I was totally lacking. At half-time Bearzot said to me, 'Stop – get yourself ready.' He was really good about it. He meant: 'Get yourself ready for the next game.' He didn't say, 'Stop and we'll see.' So hearing those words was important – to know that in the next game you would be part of the plan."

Italy managed to get out of their group without winning a match, drawing against Poland, Cameroon and Peru. Next it was Argentina, whom they beat 2-1, and then Brazil.

"A friend of mine from Vicenza brought me this coral necklace the day before the Brazil game. He said, 'Put it on, you'll see it will bring you luck.' So in the end I put it on. He'd also said to me, 'You'll score three goals.' It was incredible. I scored all three Italian goals. Those three goals took Italy to the semi-final.

"I needed a goal, because as a striker that's all that's required of you.

The first goal was ... well, from that moment on really, my life on the pitch changed ... it changed off the pitch too, but on the pitch definitely yes because it was that injection of faith that I needed. That first goal that I headed against Brazil was probably the most important goal of my whole career. The second and third goals helped but the first one was the one that really mattered.

↑ **Altobelli celebrates Rossi's goal.**

"I went back to Brazil in 1987, five years after that World Cup, and they called me "Carrasco", which means the executioner. I was in a taxi in São Paulo and the driver recognised me in his mirror. He made me get out of the taxi: 'Please get out. I can't drive you.' So I had to get out.

"But fortunately there wasn't even time to celebrate because in the World Cup you play a game every four or five days so when you win a game you immediately start thinking about the next one. We played against Poland in the semi-final. I scored another two goals in that game – by that point I was flying. It was as though someone had touched me with a magic wand and said, 'Now's your moment. Go and do what you have to do.'

"Life changes, in one week, in the blink of an eye: from a washout, which I was before, I became a phenomenon. Everything you've done up to the day of the final is not enough – it counts for nothing; the important thing is to win.

"It was a long day. Sandro Pertini, our President, came to see us. He gave us a load of tips that morning in the hotel, in a very nice way. They were like the tips you get from your coach when you're a boy and you've just started playing football: 'Be careful of those bigger than you, they'll kick you. I'm telling you, Rossi, quick, zippy, you've got to run through them ...' I said, 'Yes, Mr President, I hope to do just that!'

"You start two or three hours before to enter mentally into the game. When you're getting changed, that's when the concentration becomes very intense.

"We only saw our German opponents in the tunnel ten minutes before coming out for the game. It's not that you fear them – you don't let on anything – but you realise that they're there and they're pretty big! Inside myself I was saying, 'No, we are stronger, we are superior, we *feel* stronger ... we have to show it.' Physically they were bigger but we knew we were stronger technically.

"I scored the first goal. I set off a tenth of a second before my marker, before the ball was struck. You don't go because you've thought about it; you go because it's instinctive. You know that, out of 20 of those balls, you won't get 18 or 19 of them, but there will be that one time when you get it, and so you have to go, and you have to go with the conviction that you'll get there first.

I stole a tenth of a second on my opponent and I got there first with a header.

"The second goal by [Marco] Tardelli was a beautiful goal. It was a goal which showed the team at its best. It was a goal where we had seven or eight passes, built things up, moves, skill – that goal had everything – and so you can't say we sat back and waited for them. By that point we were better than Germany. Tardelli truly exploded there.

"We led the game. It was only really the third goal by [Alessandro] Altobelli that was a goal off a counter-attack.

"When the referee blew the final whistle, then you don't immediately realise what you've just done. You're living this thing on the pitch with your team-mates, but you don't understand the enormity of the victory. Like I said, your entire world, your nation, every Italian are watching.

"During the game you think about nothing else but afterwards you have time to take it in. You see the sea of Italian flags. I started to think about home, about my father, all the people who had wished me well and helped me. I got some flashbacks of when I was a boy playing.

"I started to think about all of this. In the end you say 'I did it'."

From being a disgrace Rossi became a national hero. While he had a successful club career at Juventus FC, AC Milan and Hellas Verona FC, he will always be remembered for the 1982 FIFA World Cup™. He retired from football in 1987 and now owns a vineyard and olive grove in Tuscany.

1982

Marco
TARDELLI

TEAM	**Italy**
BORN	**24 September 1954**
THE MATCH	**In 1982 the FIFA World Cup™ was hosted by Spain. The final was played on 11 July in the Estadio Santiago Bernabéu, Madrid.**
ATTENDANCE	**90,000**
RESULT	**Italy 3-1 West Germany**
THE GOAL	**Tardelli scored Italy's second goal in the 69th minute.**
PHOTOGRAPHED	**at San Lorenzo Restaurant, London**

By the time Tardelli went to Spain in 1982, he was a well-established first-team player, with experience at Juventus FC, where he had won the Serie A title four times, and with Italy, with whom he had been to the FIFA World Cup™ Finals in Argentina in 1978. He was more of a defensive midfielder than an attacking one.

"I started playing football aged about six. We used to play on a field that belonged to the church. Before we played, we had to go to mass – I was an altar boy – or else the priest wouldn't let us use the field. We didn't have any kit or boots, so I played in my normal shoes, which always got me into trouble. My parents were against me playing football. They wanted me to study, but I was lucky: I had three older brothers, two of whom loved football, so they would do summer jobs and give me money so I could play football. I'm very grateful. I was the youngest. My mother was hoping for a girl. She burnt my kit once because she didn't want me to be a footballer. By 1973 I was a professional. Until I won the World Cup I never realised I was a good player.

"My debut for Italy took place on 1 April 1976. April Fool's Day! I never thought I was a great player, I just wanted to play. I played in the World Cup in Argentina. It was incredible. We beat Argentina, who went on to become champions. That was a great Italian team. I don't think we were any better in 1982 but we were more united.

"The first World Cup I saw was in 1970. We didn't have a television at home and so I managed to watch it at the restaurant where I was working by sneaking off between serving courses. I had a great time. The owner had less of a great time but I enjoyed myself. When I saw [Roberto] Boninsegna's equaliser against Brazil [see pages 66-71] I went crazy. The hotel owner wasn't too pleased. He made me pay for it later.

"I arrived in Spain in '82 in bad shape, because I was very tired by the end of the season, plus in '82 I was coming back from an injury. At first, I shared a room with [Claudio] Gentile but he only stayed two nights because I never slept and I got on his nerves. He liked his sleep. He got himself another room and nobody wanted to share with me, so I had a room on my own.

↓ **Tardelli scores Italy's second goal in the 69th minute.**

"After the first couple of games I started to improve, get in gear and play well, up to the point that I managed to score two goals. They were nice goals but, although personally I remember my goal against Argentina better than the one in the final, everyone else remembers the one in the final. The semi-final against Poland was quite easy.

"We stopped talking to the press completely because they were printing stories that just weren't true. We nominated Dino Zoff to talk to them and the rest of us were silent. It helped unite us.

"We were a very united side. We helped one other.

We were always very aware of any mistakes any of us had made so we made sure we protected one another. This was a lovely thing – it should be like that in life in general.

"We beat a Brazil team that was, in my opinion, the strongest side they'd ever had – apart from the 1970 team, that is. After that we thought we could beat anyone. I had to come off in that game because I got injured. I didn't know if I'd play again in the tournament.

"The night before the final was like any other night. I went to Zoff and [Gaetano] Scirea's room to talk and calm down, but I couldn't sleep. I really thought about everything that had happened in my life: my mother who didn't want me to play, my brothers who helped me to play ... All sorts of things come into your mind then ... even thoughts of funny things: if I won the World Cup, would my friends back at home still talk to me. Little things.

↑ **Tardelli's celebration has come to epitomise what it must feel like to score in a World Cup Final.**

"I remember very well actually striking my goal. I was lucky I was in the right place and was able to put it in the back of the net.

"It was Scirea who gave me that lovely pass.

I could kiss him – he's in heaven now but it will still get there. He gave me this ball, which I didn't stop as I meant to. It went a bit long and I had to slide to reach it and I managed to strike it well.

"I believe when someone scores a goal in a World Cup Final there is never an exaggerated way to celebrate.

"I think in that moment I went beyond madness.

"I saw the ball go in the net. And when I saw it … it was incredible. One thing I did feel though – among all those people, my team-mates, in that moment I isolated myself. I felt alone and it was lovely. It was a feeling I'd never had before but in that moment when I scored I was completely alone … and during the celebration too. It was a very personal thing. I couldn't hear a thing – there was no one around me anymore. It was like being in a silent film. They tried to stop me but they couldn't catch me. It was a very strange but very beautiful thing.

"A lot of things went through my mind … because you see your life, you see all the sacrifices you made. Certainly, when I scored, I saw my youth, my parents, my brothers, all the things I'd gone through to reach that moment. They are flashes.

"I was very tired when I came back to the centre circle. I had trouble breathing too. I made the sign of the cross because I think I said some things that weren't nice to say so I crossed myself. It's the last goal I ever scored for Italy.

"What has remained inside of me is this solitude.

It's not a solitude that implies unhappiness. Instead, it was absolute ecstasy, happiness lived out alone. I was with the others but I was alone because I couldn't hear anything … It's difficult to describe. It's true – there is no doubt that man is born alone and dies alone.

"The night after the game absolutely nothing happened. Everyone went out; but me, Scirea and Rossi, I think, stayed in our rooms in the hotel talking. Scirea was an outstanding person. I went to his room and he was reading. We started talking, saying, 'Just think, we're World Cup champions.' It was very peaceful."

"The morning of the final, I can't say I woke up because I hadn't slept. Like every other morning we all had breakfast together. There was a deep silence. On the day of any game, I remember, we had this thing and we were always very quiet. Internally, everyone was going through his own game. We said hello to each other but we were quiet … calm.

"Arriving at the stadium was very emotional; it made your spine tingle because for us it was like walking into a shrine.

"The first half of the game was quite strange … difficult. Each side was studying the other side. We had this great chance with [Antonio] Cabrini's penalty but he missed it. It was at that moment that I understood we could maybe win the World Cup because none of us got upset with Cabrini; rather, we helped keep up his morale because he had a ten-minute dip after because he'd lost his nerve. Anyway, it was an ugly first half, not a beautiful one. I've watched footage of it since and it was quite boring.

"We came out strong for the second half.

[Paolo] Rossi's goal was a goal of cunning, of quickness. A goal of a player who's very good in the area.

"To see Pertini [Alessandro Pertini, Italian President 1978-85] cheering, raising his arms, telling the King of Spain that the game was over and there was no way they could catch us now … that made us very proud.

Tardelli's celebration upon scoring his goal remains one of the most iconic moments in FIFA World Cup™ history. It seems to take a moment for what has just happened to sink in, but when it does his celebration epitomises what every person who has ever dreamed of scoring a goal in the FIFA World Cup™ Final must imagine. In 2014 his celebration was named the fourth greatest FIFA World Cup™ moment of all time by the BBC.

Tardelli retired from playing in 1988 and has had several management posts including most recently assisting Giovanni Trapattoni with the Republic of Ireland.

1982

Alessandro
ALTOBELLI

TEAM	**Italy**
BORN	**28 November 1955**
THE MATCH	**In 1982 the FIFA World Cup™ was hosted by Spain. The final was played on 11 July in the Estadio Santiago Bernabéu, Madrid.**
ATTENDANCE	**90,000**
RESULT	**Italy 3-1 West Germany**
THE GOAL	**In the 81st minute Altobelli scored Italy's third goal.**
PHOTOGRAPHED	**at the television station where he works in Milan**

The Italian team that went to Spain were a more mature version of the one that had come fourth in the 1978 Cup final in Argentina. Expectations were high.

"I was born in a small village, Sonnino [Lazio], that didn't even have a sports field. My father wanted me to be a butcher so I did that. I'd get up at 4am and I'd get home at 7.30pm. Our local butcher was starting a football team so he asked me to come and work for him as well as to play for his team, so I did that. We were really good. It never entered my head that I could play in Serie A [Italy's top league], let alone play for Italy. If there are dreams, there are disappointments. I didn't allow myself to dream.

"In 1982 I had had a good season with Inter [Milan]. I'd scored a lot of goals, so Bearzot [Enzo Bearzot, Italy manager 1975-86] was aware of me.

"You get the news about the call-up from the club. They call the club, not you. I'd been at Inter since 1976. I'd scored a lot of goals but I'd never been called up. I played once in 1980 but that was it.

"Enzo Bearzot, besides being a great coach, I think he is a great man.

"You had to prove yourself. When someone got called up, very rarely would he let that player go. I arrived in the national team in '80 and I left in '88. When Bearzot called you, he didn't leave you; he supported you, even in tough times. I shared a room with [Giuseppe] Dossena, who was a Torino FC player, a midfielder. He didn't have the same luck as me because he was always on the bench. He never got a game.

"My father and my mother lived in a village and watched [the World Cup] on television. My mother didn't really watch the games because she was scared.

"I was in the team but I was going to be on the bench. I knew that. You still prepare yourself in the same way. You may not be in the starting line-up but the moment you're told to go on you have to be on the same wavelength as the team."

Italy managed to get out of the group stages without a win, drawing against Poland, Peru and Cameroon. Next they beat Argentina 2-1 and then Brazil 3-2.

"After we beat Brazil, we knew what good form we were in. There wasn't much in our way after that. In the semi-final against Poland, Ciccio Graziani injured his shoulder, so I got to go on for about half an hour.

"The evening before the Cup final, we were ready. It was hard to get to sleep early but we were focused, we knew what we had to do. Of course, I had a dream. And my dream was of maybe being able to get on the pitch, to play a good part of the game. At that point I wasn't playing. We had [Paolo] Rossi and Graziani in the starting line-up so I was out.

"The Bernabéu was divided with a fence: we were on one side and the Germans on the other. It was like having a lion and a tiger who look at each other but they can't get at each other because they're separated.

"We looked at them. We studied them. We tried to make out what mood they were in. We tried to see if they were scared.

We tried to make out what they were feeling because, truly, we felt good and we wanted to pick up some sign. I respected them. I always respected them and I still respect them today for what they did, but in no way did I fear them. I wasn't scared of anyone.

"The game started and I was on the bench with the others. When I saw Graziani go down, I saw him touch his shoulder. It was a split second. I got out of the dugout, took off my tracksuit and said 'This is my moment.' I didn't wait for Bearzot to call me because maybe at that moment he might have thought of someone else.

↓ **Altobelli makes it 3-0 to Italy in the 81st minute.**

"... I'd seen him [Graziani] in training and I knew that he wasn't right. I was super ready. In fact, if you look at the footage, when Graziani fell seven minutes into the final, before he'd even got up I was already on the pitch because I'd already taken everything off, I was ready for the substitution.

"Of course, I wasn't wishing him to get injured, but I welcomed the chance to get on the pitch, to play, to win, to score, to become a World Cup champion.

"I passed the ball to Bruno Conti. He went into the area and they fouled him, which got the penalty.

"[Antonio] Cabrini was up for it. He went to the penalty spot and missed. Here, once again, Bearzot was good. At half-time I remember Cabrini burst into tears. Bearzot calmed him down, 'We'll win. You'll see.'

"Even after Tardelli's second goal it was 2-0, straight away I was back in position ready to counter and ready to attack again. It couldn't finish 2-0 – I had it in my head to leave my mark.

↑ **Altobelli and West Germany's Bernd Foerster race for the ball.**

"So when I saw that Bruno Conti had started a counter-attack down on the right wing, I started to move. I saw that Germany's defence was a bit uneven. He [Conti] went into the area and passed me the ball. The first thing I did was look straight away at [Harald] Schumacher and he was coming for me. I was a bit quicker than Schumacher.

That noise the net makes when you strike the goal, few people know it.

Maybe the goalkeeper knows it, but he never wants to hear it. But the striker understands it well. It was the feeling I was searching for. It was the ideal moment to close the game. It was the ideal moment to seal it. It was the ideal moment to leave my mark.

"It's the squad that wins ... the squad as a group that wins. If team members play for one other, you can get a result. If each man is playing for himself, you've already lost."

Altobelli had a glittering career at Inter Milan, winning the Coppa Italia in 1978 and again in 1982. He joined Juventus FC in 1987 for a season. He retired from playing in 1990 after a season with Brescia Calcio in Serie B. He briefly tried to enter politics. He is now a TV pundit with global network beIN Sports.

Paul
BREITNER

TEAM: West Germany

BORN: 5 September 1951

THE MATCH: In 1982 the FIFA World Cup™ was hosted by Spain. The final was played on 11 July in the Estadio Santiago Bernabéu, Madrid.

ATTENDANCE: 90,000

RESULT: Italy 3-1 West Germany

THE GOAL: Breitner scored the goal in the 83rd minute.

PHOTOGRAPHED at Olympiastadion, Munich.

Although the score was 0-0 at half-time the Italians took control in the second half with goals from Rossi, Tardelli and Altobelli. Breitner had scored a crucial penalty to help West Germany win the FIFA World Cup™ in 1974 but by the time he scored in 1982 the final was all but over and it was little more than a consolation goal. His goal did, however, mean that he joined Vavá, Pelé and Zidane, as the only people to have scored in more than one FIFA World Cup™ Final.

In 1998 he was announced as the German International Coach but the DFB (German Football Federation) changed their mind 17 hours later, deciding he was too controversial a figure and gaining him the nickname the 17 Hour Bundestrainer. He now works as a pundit and columnist.

see also pages 94-9

1986

José Luis ("Tata")
BROWN

TEAM	**Argentina**
BORN	**10 November 1956**
THE MATCH	**In 1986 the FIFA World Cup™ was hosted by Mexico. The final was played on 29 June in the Estadio Azteca, Mexico City.**
ATTENDANCE	**114,600**
RESULT	**Argentina 3-2 West Germany**
THE GOAL	**In the 23rd minute Brown scored the first Argentine goal.**
PHOTOGRAPHED	**at home in Buenos Aires**

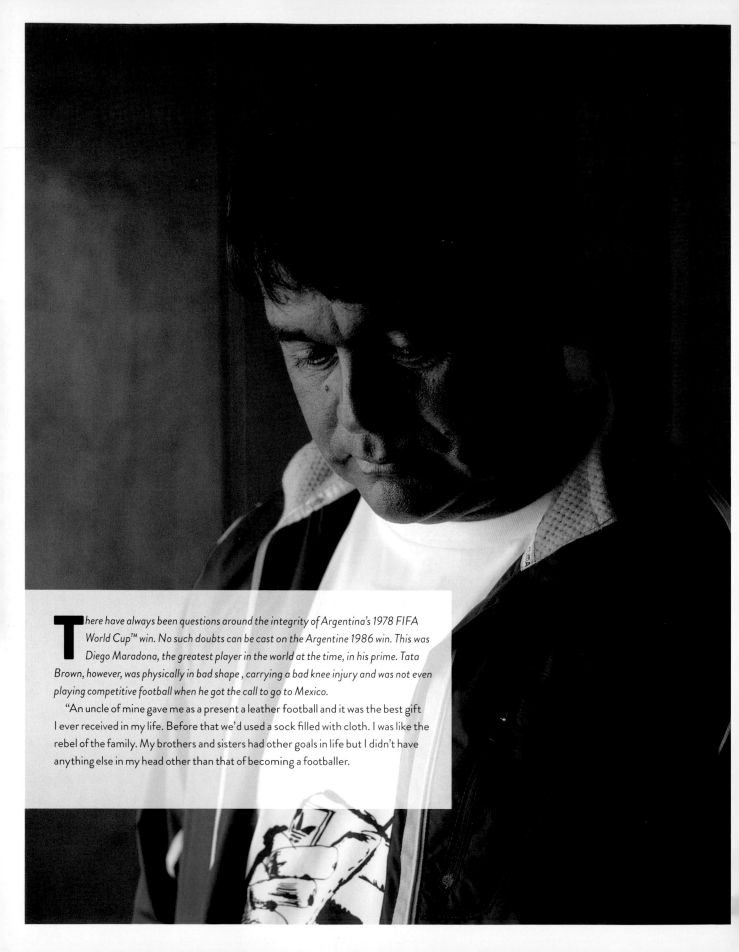

There have always been questions around the integrity of Argentina's 1978 FIFA World Cup™ win. No such doubts can be cast on the Argentine 1986 win. This was Diego Maradona, the greatest player in the world at the time, in his prime. Tata Brown, however, was physically in bad shape , carrying a bad knee injury and was not even playing competitive football when he got the call to go to Mexico.

"An uncle of mine gave me as a present a leather football and it was the best gift I ever received in my life. Before that we'd used a sock filled with cloth. I was like the rebel of the family. My brothers and sisters had other goals in life but I didn't have anything else in my head other than that of becoming a footballer.

"When we went to Mexico I didn't have a club. I had a serious knee injury and Deportivo Español just said they didn't want me any more so I wasn't at any club. Fortunately, Bilardo [Carlos Bilardo, Argentina manager 1983-90] had known me since I was 18, so he knew what I was capable of; but the knee problem was serious. I only went to Mexico as the substitute for Daniel Passarella.

"Look, let me explain, when we left Argentina to go to Mexico, we were all alone. There was absolutely nobody to say goodbye, only a couple of our wives, but in general terms, nobody.

"There were some Argentine journalists who had bought return plane tickets and only rented rooms for the first round, because everybody was saying that we could not be participants in a World Cup because of our qualifying games and how we were playing. It was an incredible thing, incredible, the lack of support.

"It turned out Passarella had some problem and I had to play the first match. I was really nervous. When we lined up with the Koreans and they played the national anthems, my legs were shaking.

"The team physio was Professor Ricardo Echeverría, a guy who for all of us was more than a professor – he was like a father. He was the man who, each Sunday at 10am, would come pick me up, take me to training; he was always close to me, he would always talk to me, he would always advise me."

Argentina progressed comfortably out of their group beating South Korea and drawing with Italy. The most difficult match they had was against England in the quarter-final. In that match Maradona scored both Argentine goals. The first he punched into the net, a goal that became known as "The Hand of God", and the second four minutes later when he dribbled around five English players. Argentina saw off Belgium in the semi-final 2-0. Having been brought along as a substitute, Brown played in every match from start to finish.

↓ **José Luis Brown and Oscar Ruggeri jump for the ball.**

"The night before the World Cup Final I did not sleep. I was tossing and turning in my bed, staring at the ceiling, looking at my kids' pictures.

"Knowing that in five, six hours you are going to play a World Cup Final gives you a feeling that's very hard to explain. We were all in the same situation, you know. We were all silent – and it's an amazing silence because there was total concentration. I remember Bilardo saying, 'We've reached this point, and if you this let this pass by, after all we've been through, it would be a terrible shame.'

"On the bus we would play a song by Sergio Denis, an Argentine singer. The song was 'Big Giant', which is about a father talking to his son. That was very emotional for us. Bear in mind that at that point we had left our home 70 days before. We would always get off the bus in the same order. [Oscar] Ruggeri would get off the bus with a very big stereo and the *Rocky* song would be playing. We would all go into the changing rooms jumping and screaming. It was really crazy.

"When we came out of the changing rooms the Germans were there. We could see their concentration. Diego [Maradona] had his fists clenched and was shouting, "Come on, come on!" It was very intense.

"My goal ... how can I say it ? ...it has changed my identity.

You have no idea of how proud I feel of having scored a goal for my country in a World Cup Final.

"Diego came in front of me and the referee blew the whistle for a free kick. Burru[chaga] hit the ball really hard ... and with a curve! So when I started sprinting I looked at Schumacher and I said to myself, 'He's not going to make it,' because of the way the ball was doing the curve. So the only thing I had in front of me was Diego. So I rushed up, pushing Diego over, and headed the ball ... and it went in. I didn't see the ball go in. I headed it and when it landed I ran off to celebrate.

"But we made mistakes and got tied at 2-2."

Argentina looked certain victors, up 2-0 with only 17 minutes to play. Germany managed to pull two back with just ten minutes remaining. Three minutes later Maradona set up Jorge Burruchaga to score the winner.

"Thank God for Diego, Burru and [Jorge] Valdano's stroke of genius and everybody else who made the third goal, and right away we knew we had it won.

"I hugged Marcelo Trobbiani and went to run the lap of honour, and at that moment, when I'd run for about 30 metres, I remembered Professor Echeverría, and I ran back to see him. He was in midfield standing, crying.

"So I grabbed him and told him: 'Prof, come with me to do the lap of honour.' He was saying, 'No, no!' so I told him, 'Come with me and do the lap. Listen to me I am here because of you.' We hugged each other and Marcelo joined us in the hug and then three of us did a lap of honour at the Azteca Stadium.

"It was very emotional.

There are no words ... no words.

"A few years ago we were on our way to play in the Olympic Games in Beijing with the Argentine U-23 team. We had to wait for four hours [for a connecting flight] in Washington, DC. There were some airport employees there and we had a coffee with them. One of them came up to me and asked me for a picture. So I told the guy: 'Look at the players that are here – [Lionel] Messi, [Javier] Mascherano and [Fernando] Gago – and you are going to take a picture with me?' And the guy said, 'Yes – you scored a goal in a World Cup Final!'"

↑ **José Luis Brown heads the ball to score Argentina's first goal of the match.**

Brown went to play in Europe – for Brest and Real Murcia – after the
World Cup before a brief stint with the Argentine club Racing. He retired
from playing in 1989. He had several assistant manager jobs including
assisting Bilardo at Boca Juniors. He lives in Buenos Aires.

1986

Jorge
VALDANO

TEAM	**Argentina**
BORN	**4 October 1955**
THE MATCH	**In 1986 the FIFA World Cup™ was hosted by Mexico. The final was played on 29 June in the Estadio Azteca, Mexico City.**
ATTENDANCE	**114,600**
RESULT	**Argentina 3-2 West Germany**
THE GOAL	**In the 55th minute Valdano scored Argentina's second goal.**
PHOTOGRAPHED	**at Estadio Santiago Bernabéu, Madrid**

Argentina were in disarray when they arrived in Mexico. With poor recent results, infighting and a lack of faith among both the fans and the press, Argentina seemed to have poor prospects. They were a team, however, of brilliant individuals, most notably, of course, Diego Maradona. In 1986 Valdano had been playing in Spain for 11 years, most recently with Real Madrid, with whom he had won the UEFA Cup twice, in 1985 and 1986. Valdano scored in both finals.

Argentina came through the group stage easily. Their first real challenge was meeting England in the quarter-final. In that match Maradona scored twice. The first was the infamous "Hand of God" goal where he punched the ball into the net. For the second he took the ball from the halfway line and single-handedly beat five England players before scoring. It is considered one of the greatest solo goals ever scored.

"The game against England was tough. I made the run with Maradona when he scored his second goal. He received a difficult ball in the centre circle. I started my run as a player and finished it as a spectator. I was dazzled by the beauty of what I was seeing. If he had passed to me at the end, I would have missed. It was like I was hypnotised.

"I had had to play in the UEFA Cup final against FC Köln in Germany so I was late joining the team. I hadn't been in Argentina but I was very aware of the contempt the fans and the press felt for us. We'd played badly in the preliminary games, so we arrived with lots of doubts. Mentally, I was very strong. I had just won the league title and the UEFA Cup with Real Madrid. Physically I was beaten up but psychologically I was good.

"In our first match, against Korea, I scored in the sixth minute and that really helped our confidence. The Argentine team of '86 was peculiar. It was the most spectacular psychological transformation I have ever seen. We were worried about playing South Korea, and a month later we had no doubts about beating Germany in the final.

"I can describe the last night before the final perfectly well, because I did not sleep, not even one minute. It was the day I had been waiting for my whole life. I was worried though I knew I needed to sleep if I was going to be in peak physical condition.

"I would think: 'Am I actually living this?' I felt very privileged.

"We had become quite superstitious and had to listen to two songs on the bus on the way to the ground. I can't remember what they were but they were pretty terrible. We had to listen to them every time.

"At that time the European game was more physical, more tactical, whereas the South Americans were more about flair and skills. I had been playing in Madrid in Spain so I understood the European way.

"The ball was heading towards Maradona, so I ran diagonally towards the left side of the field. Maradona gave it to [Héctor] Enrique, and just at the moment I was passing to the centre field, Enrique passed it to me. When I got onto [Harald] Schumacher I positioned myself practically in profile so as to open both angles.

"If he closed the second post, I could dribble past him, if not just shoot ... And, well ... I chose to shoot, a very close shot on the post, relatively smooth. And when I knew it went in, it was like 'Is it true, or is it a lie?' ... 'Is this the real world, or am I just having that old dream of mine in which I am scoring a goal in a World Cup?' You're afraid that your mother will wake you up!

"The mistake is thinking that the game is over. At some time during the game I looked at the stands and said, 'You are a World Cup champion.' But we were playing against Germany and the discipline of the Germans and how they react to this kind of situation was well known in World Cup football. The truth is they really gave us a scare.

"[Jorge] Burruchaga, who was the calmest of all, a player who doesn't talk much, said, 'Are you OK?' 'Yes, yes, we are OK.' 'OK,' he said, 'we are going to win ... We are going to win.' He was convinced that we were going to overcome that situation. Maradona kicked to Burruchaga, and Burruchaga ran and I went along beside him, keeping

↑ **Valdano scores Argentina's second goal in the 55th minute.**

him company. Every time I meet him in Buenos Aires I tell him, 'You still haven't seen me?'

"Well, the feeling was that that was the definitive goal. There wasn't much time left until the final whistle, but I must say that they were the longest minutes of my life.

"I did have a lap of honour. When I saw that I was close to the changing room, I immediately went to enjoy my loneliness, and slowly the rest started arriving. Most of them were crying. When I arrived at the changing rooms I thought I had to cry.

It was the culminating moment of my life, and I couldn't cry ... I couldn't cry.

"Two or three years later, my family got into the habit of sending me tapes from Argentina with messages and music. I would play the tape on my Walkman and go jogging in the park. Once my brother included the narration of my goal by an Argentine football commentator whom we knew from watching football as children. So when I was running I started listening to the goal, and I couldn't stop crying. I had to hide because I was crying so much, crying with happiness at winning the World Cup."

Valdano was named La Liga Foreign Player of the Year in 1986. A year after his World Cup win he was struck down with hepatitis and forced to retire. He recovered well but it finished his career. Nicknamed "The Philosopher", he went on to write or edit two books on football. In 1994 he became coach at his old club, Real Madrid, where he won the league. He left for a season at Valencia CF before returning to Real Madrid as Director of Football. He left permanently in 2011.

Karl-Heinz
RUMMENIGGE

TEAM	**West Germany**
BORN	**25 September 1955**
THE MATCH	**In 1986 the FIFA World Cup™ was hosted by Mexico. The final was played on 29 June in the Estadio Azteca, Mexico City.**
ATTENDANCE	**114,600**
RESULT	**Argentina 3-2 West Germany**
THE GOAL	**In the 74th minute Rummenigge scored West Germany's first goal.**
PHOTOGRAPHED	**at FC Bayern Munich grounds**

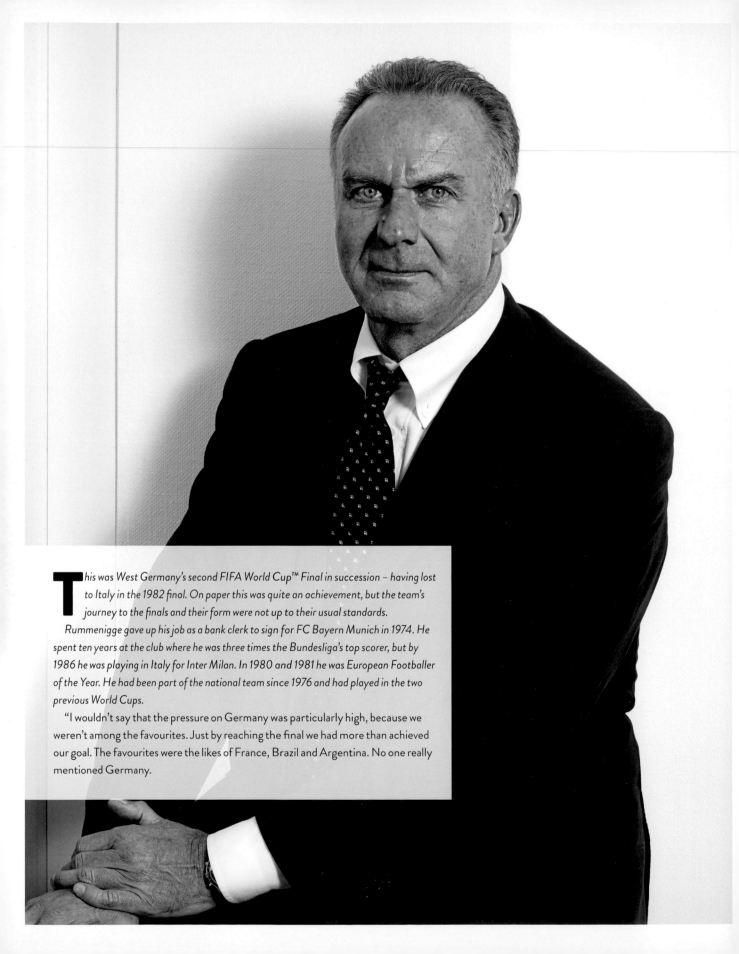

This was West Germany's second FIFA World Cup™ Final in succession – having lost to Italy in the 1982 final. On paper this was quite an achievement, but the team's journey to the finals and their form were not up to their usual standards.

Rummenigge gave up his job as a bank clerk to sign for FC Bayern Munich in 1974. He spent ten years at the club where he was three times the Bundesliga's top scorer, but by 1986 he was playing in Italy for Inter Milan. In 1980 and 1981 he was European Footballer of the Year. He had been part of the national team since 1976 and had played in the two previous World Cups.

"I wouldn't say that the pressure on Germany was particularly high, because we weren't among the favourites. Just by reaching the final we had more than achieved our goal. The favourites were the likes of France, Brazil and Argentina. No one really mentioned Germany.

"We won the first match against Scotland, drew with Uruguay and narrowly lost the third to Denmark. We had a mixed start, but when the knockout competition started, we improved from match to match.

"I can remember Franz Beckenbauer's [Germany manager 1984-90] words when we played against Morocco in the last 16. He came to my room and said: 'Today we have to win because we can't be eliminated by Morocco [generally considered a poor team].'

"Then, when we played against Mexico, he said: 'Well, this is the host. Hmm, this will be difficult.'

"But then we stayed in the tournament and by reaching the final we had more than achieved our goal. It was already mission accomplished.

"On the day of the final, we were woken at six in the morning, as the match was at midday local time in Mexico City, due to the time difference. We had brunch with pasta for breakfast and all the frills. Then we left for the stadium at 9am.

"It was incredibly hot and damp. We arrived at the stadium about an hour and a half before the match. It was already almost full. It was an overwhelming spectacle. There were already about 100.000 people in the stadium. There were people of all races from Latin America, from Europe, from all over the world. I knew before the match that it would be my last match for Germany, because I felt that I had reached an age where I should end my career, at least at international level.

"So we had a pretty strange preparation. As we stood in the centre circle at midday, it was 40°C [104°F] in the shade and you couldn't see your own shadow.

"Well, after it was 2-0, I felt it was over, because the Argentines seemed to have a very well-organised defence and we couldn't find a way through. Then we were lucky, in that Beckenbauer, the coach, had the right idea when he brought on Dieter Hoeneß, who was physically a very strong player. The Argentine defence had trouble coping with this giant. He played centre forward, and towards the end of the match we played literally with three forwards.

"I can remember how I went forward, just randomly after a corner, and the ball was flicked on by the player that stood at the near post. I think it was Dieter. I was lucky enough to reach the ball before the defender. I took a long step, there was a sort of sliding tackle and the ball went into the goal.

"I immediately took the ball to the centre circle and punched my hand with my fist and said,

'Guys, now we have another chance. Let's try again to turn the match around.'

"And that's what happened: Rudi Völler scored the equalising goal and the world seemed upside down again.

"And suddenly anything was possible. They [the Argentines] were really scared of losing the match. Then we made a major tactical mistake. I think there were eight minutes left when Rudi scored. We should have organised ourselves in defence and played for extra time. I saw it coming, because we had the ball and were attacking, then they counter-attacked. The Argentines played brilliantly.

"And when [Jorge] Burruchaga ran towards our goal, I knew it was a goal. I was appalled. I saw the whole thing coming seconds in advance. *Finito*, game over, we had lost.

"But, to be fair, I have to say that it simply wasn't supposed to happen, and you can't help it and you have to accept it."

↑ **Rummenigge pulls one back for West Germany in the 74th minute.**

Rummenigge retired from international football after the 1986 FIFA World Cup™ and from playing football in 1989 while playing for Servette FC in Geneva, Switzerland. He is currently chairman at FC Bayern Munich as well as of the European Club Association and is a member of the UEFA strategic advisory committee for professional football.

1986

Rudi VÖLLER

TEAM	**West Germany**
BORN	**13 April 1960**
THE MATCH	**In 1986 the FIFA World Cup™ was hosted by Mexico. The final was played on 29 June in the Estadio Azteca, Mexico City.**
ATTENDANCE	**114,600**
RESULT	**Argentina 3-2 West Germany**
THE GOAL	**In the 80th minute Völler equalised for West Germany.**
PHOTOGRAPHED	**at the Bayer 04 Leverkusen grounds**

I n 1986 Rudolf "Rudi" Völler – nicknamed "Tante Käthe" [Aunty Kathy] because of his hairstyle – was the Bundesliga's top scorer with SV Werder Bremen. He had made his international debut against Northern Ireland in 1982.

"We hadn't been playing that well in the qualifiers or the warm-up matches. It's remarkable we got to the final at all. We didn't feel that much pressure because we were definitely the underdogs.

"We only finished second in our group to Denmark. We had lost to them. They were a very strong team. We then managed to beat Morocco, but it wasn't beautiful football. Then it was the Mexicans, and they were favourites because they were at home and had the home support. We were getting better all the time and we deserved to beat them on penalties. And, then again, we weren't expected to beat France. They had just beaten Brazil. We beat them and somehow found ourselves in the final.

"It was tense but we knew we had nothing to lose. Argentina had played amazing football. This was Diego Maradona's World Cup. He was the star of the whole World Cup.

"To be fair, even though towards the end it was pretty close, we lost against a very, very good Argentine team.

"We knew we were a good team, but we didn't go as far as to think of becoming World Cup champions.

"After the first goal, they were in the lead 1-0 until the half-time break. You are still in with a chance to equalise, but we had very few scoring chances.

"At 2-0 down, it was getting difficult. Although you still believe a little bit, you are well aware of the fact that it's getting difficult. This has always been one of our strengths, not only at that World Cup, but a strength of the Germans in general; you should never write us off.

"[Andreas] Brehme took the corner. We had practised these before. I was standing at the near post and I managed to flick the ball on to "Kalle" Rummenigge, who kicked the ball into the goal from a few metres.

"At that moment, we knew that we would have another chance.

↓ **Völler scores in the 80th minute.**

"Thomas Berthold gets the header and heads the ball back to the so-called danger area. And then I got the header. I was standing exactly in the right place at the right time, and

from a few metres distance I headed the ball into the net. It was beautiful.

"Once we caught up, everyone thought, 'If we make it to extra time, we will be World Cup champions.'

The Argentines were demoralised, they were a bit tired, and I think we all agree that, if we had gone into extra time, we would have won.

"We played a very offensive game in the seven, eight minutes still to go. We wanted to win the match 3-2. This was our basic mistake. Franz Beckenbauer [West Germany manager 1984-90] substituted an offensive player. It was logical because we had to turn the game around. That was fatal.

"We should have ... because the Argentines had had a shock, they were knackered ... we should have simply played for extra time.

"It was a counter-attack. We had been pressing forward the whole time and what happened was – I have to say it was a sort of mirror image of the whole tournament – Diego Maradona, even though at that point he was pretty tired, did this brilliant pass to [Jorge] Burruchaga. I was hoping Hans-Peter Briegel, who was our fastest player at the time, would catch him, but he didn't make it.

"Yes, there were still a few minutes to go, [but] as much as the Argentines had had their shock, now we had had ours. It was just too late. The Argentines played very intelligently, they had a good defence, and then it was over.

We tried everything we could, we almost had it,

but at the end of the day the Argentines were simply the better team in the final and they deserved to be World Cup champions."

↑ **Völler equalises for West Germany with ten minutes remaining.**

After the FIFA World Cup™ Völler went to play at AS Roma in Italy where he stayed until 1992. He played briefly in France for Olympique de Marseille before returning to Germany to play for Bayer 04 Leverkusen and retired in 1996. He was part of the 1990 German World Cup–winning team and then won the 2002 FIFA World Cup™ as the German manager. He is currently Sporting Director at Bayer 04 Leverkusen.

1986

MEXICO86
© FIFA TM

Jorge
BURRUCHAGA

TEAM	**Argentina**
BORN	**9 October 1962**
THE MATCH	**In 1986 the FIFA World Cup™ was hosted by Mexico. The final was played on 29 June in the Estadio Azteca, Mexico City.**
ATTENDANCE	**114,600**
RESULT	**Argentina 3-2 West Germany**
THE GOAL	**In the 83rd minute Burruchaga scored the winner for Argentina.**
PHOTOGRAPHED	**at the Arsenal de Sarandí grounds, Buenos Aires**

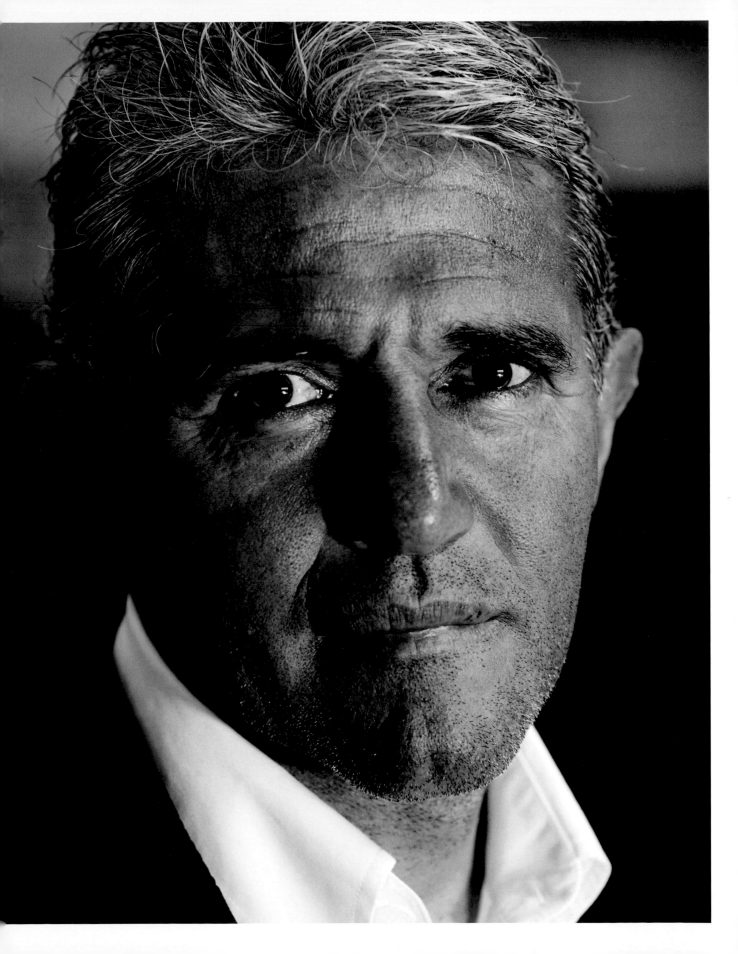

Burruchaga was playing for French team FC Nantes in 1986. The Argentines were a team of incredible individuals, but there were divisions within the team and they had not performed well in warm-up matches. This led coach Carlos Bilardo to abandon the friendlies and head to Mexico before any of the other teams. This not only helped the team sort out its differences but also gave them more time to acclimatise to the heat and altitude. Burruchaga played in midfield alongside 25-year-old team captain Diego Maradona, at the time the greatest player in the world.

"I'm from a humble family. We came to Quilmes just outside Buenos Aires when I was three so my father could look for work. I had 11 brothers and sisters. We had to work in order to eat, to have something on the table. My father was not a soccer fan. Soccer would not save you like it might do today. My father's priority was working and he wanted us to work. Work came first, soccer a definite second. In fact, we all worked. When I was seven or eight years old I started working, selling newspapers, selling ice cream or doing whatever I could to help the family.

"My mother and my brothers were the opposite. My mother loved football, she was a 100 per cent football fan, and she was one of those mothers who would take out some money so that I could go and train at the club, so that I could play football. It's because of that that I had that love, that passion, inside of me.

"She really wanted us to be able to play football and compete in the first division, so you can imagine her reaction whenever I won something with CA Independiente, let alone when we won the World Cup!

"It was not a united team. After losing a pre-tournament friendly to Atlético Nacional in Colombia, we had a team meeting that lasted over three hours. There were big personalities, jealousies, cliques, but we had great players. I don't think I'll ever see a player who can even get close to what Diego was as a football player; I don t think there will ever be another Diego. We decided to cancel our second friendly and go to Mexico and prepare. That decision made a big difference.

"I arrived at Mexico really fit, really, really well.

If you make a mistake in a World Cup, you will have no second chance."

Argentina got out of the groups with ease. Their toughest game would be against England in the quarter-finals. Maradona's second goal – after his controversial "Hand of God" goal – is considered one of the greatest World Cup goals ever scored.

"It was after the England game that we thought we might be able to win. Russia, Brazil and France had all gone out. The semi-final against Belgium was pretty straightforward.

"That day of the final was undoubtedly the happiest day in my sporting life, no doubt about it.

"The journey was short because we were really close to the Estadio Azteca. The journey was short, though it was at ant's pace. Not just because of the people around us, and the fans going to the stadium, but because we had to listen to two "good luck" songs. One was Bonnie Tyler's 'I Need a Hero' and the other one was the theme music from the film *Rocky*. We had to tell the driver to drive slowly so we had time to finish listening to both songs.

"Carlos [Bilardo] thought Lothar Matthäus would try to mark Diego out of the game, so I would have to own the midfield. He told me to keep looking over at him as he would be giving me signals as to what to do. He stressed this a lot.

"We started well. We finished the first half 1-0 and scored again at the start of the second. And that's when things started to go awry … The team, after being in a comfortable 2-0 up, got tied 2-2 while

↑ **Burruchaga scores in the 83rd minute.**

looking for that third goal. You can't afford to stall for minute against the Germans. They were right back in it with ten minutes to go. I remember we went back to the centre, with Maradona carrying the ball, shouting and all, and I said to him "Stay calm. We will go and win this." We looked at each other and that look was more than a thousand words.

"The Mexican crowd affected us a lot. That hurt us. They even celebrated the German goals.

"So a few minutes after their equaliser, the Germans came out playing an offside trick, so I ran in front of [Karl-Heinz] Förster – he was on the right side – and I went in from left to right. I gave Maradona a shout. I shouted at him that I am going alone, that they were playing for the offside, and that there was a space. Diego was capable of that, because he hadn't heard me, and, having his back to me, he turned and passed the ball right in front of me. I was coming onto it from left to right, and the keeper was far away, because I had started running from the centre of the pitch. He was about 40 metres away. I didn't see [Jorge] Valdano on the other side.

I focused on getting to the goal the fastest way possible.

Afterwards – and I've seen it a thousand of times – I took the ball twice with my left foot, and the ball would jump – the pitch was really bad.

↑ Burruchaga scores a late winner to clinch victory for Argentina.

"Schumacher [Harald Schumacher, the German keeper] came out. My intention had been to punt it over him, but he came out with his legs out forward, giving me a gap between his legs, so I punted it just in time for it go to between his legs. It's been said that I took the ball too far forward, that I struck it badly ... but it went in!

"And then comes the most exciting part: I saw the ball going in as I ran out to the right side. I saw the linesman Ulloa, who I think was from Panama [Berny Ulloa Morera is in fact Costa Rican]. I looked up at the sky, I lifted my arms, and that was probably my way of thanking God for being able to live this moment.

"At that moment I remembered my father who hadn't wanted me to play football, and it was like saying to him – because I lost my father when I was young – I was 14 years old – it was like telling him that it had been worth all that effort, the effort my mother had made, and that I was living through it, and that he couldn't be there.

"And then the first one to come near me, with what strength he had left, was Checho Batista, and he knelt right beside me, hugging me, and, with Checho's beard, it was like having Jesus right in front of me. Then Diego arrived, and Gringo [Ricardo] Giusti, and we celebrated.

"Carlos had said that, whenever we scored goals, we could not all go and celebrate, because one or two had to be in midfield just in case the other team wanted to kick-off quickly.

"Perhaps the most divine moment that I've lived was returning with Jorge Valdano to midfield, with Jorge embracing me, looking into my eyes and saying to me: 'Now, yes, we're champions of the world and nothing can change that now.'

"And then tears fell from my eyes. It's hard to find the exact words to describe that huge moment ... I was so happy.

"Carlos was superstitious so he took me off with three minutes to go. He had done the same in the quarter- and semi-finals. Marcelo Trobbiani came on, which was great for him. I was hugging everyone on the bench. We were looking at each other saying, 'World champions. Now we are world champions'."

Burruchaga returned to France after the FIFA World Cup™ where he stayed until 1992, after which he went back to his old club, CA Indepentiente, in Buenos Aires, until he retired from playing in 1998.

He managed numerous clubs including his first club, Arsenal de Sarandí, and, most recently, Atlético de Rafaela, which he left in 2016. He lives in Buenos Aires.

ITALIA'90
© FIFA TM

Andreas
BREHME

TEAM	**West Germany**
BORN	**9 November 1960**
THE MATCH	**In 1990 the FIFA World Cup™ was hosted by Italy. The final was played on 8 July in the Stadio Olimpico, Rome.**
ATTENDANCE	**73,603**
RESULT	**West Germany 1-0 Argentina**
THE GOAL	**In the 85th minute Brehme scored the winning goal from the penalty spot.**
PHOTOGRAPHED	**at Italy beim Umile restaurant, Geretsried, Bavaria**

West Germany found themselves in their third consecutive FIFA World Cup™ Final, having lost to Italy in 1982 and to Argentina in 1986. Brehme had played in the 1986 final. He was unique in that he was equally strong with both feet. Most noted for his free kicks and penalties, he generally took penalties with his more accurate right foot and free kicks with his more powerful left. Having previously played for FC Kaiserslautern and FC Bayern Munich, in 1990 he joined Inter Milan.

"I had played in the final in 1986. I think we would have won if it had gone to extra time, but no one is denying Argentina were the better team.

"I finished my apprenticeship as a motor mechanic and I passed the exam half a year in advance, because my parents said: 'Without the exam, without the certificate, we won't let you out of here.' As a young professional football player, if you get injured, you can be forced to return to your old job. I finished the apprenticeship and a week later I started my training at 1. FC Saarbrücken, who were in the second division.

"In 1990 it was after the fall of the [Berlin] Wall and there were many talks with the [former East] German players. We thought maybe [Ulf] Kirsten and [Thomas] Doll and [Mathias] Sammer would join the team later on.

"Ten or twelve of us were already playing in Italy. It was like a holiday for us. All of us knew the country and spoke the language.

"We won our opening match against Yugoslavia 4-1 and we thought we could do this thing.

"The semi-final against England in Turin was our best match. It was, in my opinion, the best match of the World Cup.

We really didn't want to have to play the Italians because they were a very strong team playing in front of their own fans, but the Argentines put them out. Even so, I still think we would have beaten Italy.

"So it turned out we had to meet Argentina in the final again, although I don't think we thought much about 1986.

"[Franz] Beckenbauer didn't say much, just to play as we had played against England and the Netherlands.

"In the final, considering that Argentina didn't have a single corner in 90 minutes, not a single scoring chance, they were obviously playing for a penalty shoot-out. Goycochea [Sergio Goycochea, the Argentine goalkeeper] was a remarkable goalkeeper, who had got them to the final from the last 16 only by way of penalty shoot-outs. It was a pity that the fans didn't get to see a good final.

"It's a pity that it was decided thanks to a penalty kick, because after 20 minutes we should have been in the lead by three or four goals to nil. But it stayed 0-0.

"Then the climax of the game came when Rudi Völler was fouled in the 83rd minute. I couldn't see it from the back. The referee blew the whistle for a penalty. Lothar [Matthäus] didn't want to shoot, but someone had to and I felt in good form. I grabbed the ball and the worst about it was that the Argentines were arguing with the referee and they kept on kicking the ball away. That went on for maybe seven, eight minutes, until I could finally shoot.

"Rudi came up to me and said: 'Andreas, please do me a favour. If you bury the ball in the net, we will be World Cup champions.'

"I said: 'I wouldn't mind if you took the shot. We would still be World Cup champions.'

"'No,' he said, 'just do me a favour, and bury the ball in the net.'

"I said: 'Thanks, I will do my best.'

"With the left foot I can shoot harder, with the right one more accurately. I didn't ask myself for one second if I was going to shoot with my left or my right foot. It was obvious: with the right foot. I knew the corner I would shoot in, and I knew that [Sergio] Goycochea had saved many penalties. He guessed the right corner. I wasn't really paying attention to Goycochea, to be honest.

I was just glad when the ball was in the net, because it was very, very narrow. It was a relief.

↑ **Brehme scores the only goal of the match from the penalty spot.**

"If you consider that billions of people are watching you shooting this penalty kick, in the end you are either the fool or the hero. So I prefer to be the hero.

"The whole team jumped on me. We felt were we would be World Cup champions because there wasn't long left.

"We had a big party that night. It was at dinner that Beckenbauer said that he was quitting and we could call him Franz from now on. I don't think I went to bed that night.

"Years later I did a charity event at Wolfsburg [city in Lower Saxony] when they played FC Bayern Munich and Goycochea was in goal. At half-time we had a penalty shoot-out and I faced him again. I decided to choose the other corner and he thought I'd choose the same corner so he went the wrong way and I scored. It was very funny."

Brehme returned to his old club, FC Kaiserslautern, in 1993 where he stayed until he retired in 1998. He then had managerial roles at Kaiserslautern, SpVgg Unterhaching and then at VfB Stuttgart. He lives in Geretsried, Germany, and is an ambassador for the German Football Association.

1998

© FIFA TM

Zinedine
ZIDANE

TEAM	**France**
BORN	**23 June 1972**
THE MATCH	**In 1998 the FIFA World Cup™ was hosted by France. The final was played on 12 July in the Stade de France, Paris.**
ATTENDANCE	**80,000**
RESULT	**France 3-0 Brazil**
THE GOAL	**Zidane scored France's first two goals in the 27th and 45th minutes.**
PHOTOGRAPHED	**at Old Trafford, Manchester**

France had neither hosted nor been in a FIFA World Cup™ Final before, their best result having been third place in 1986. The team were praised for fielding a truly multicultural team that represented an ethnically diverse nation.

In 1990 Zidane – "Zizou" – was probably the best player in the world and remains one of the greatest of all time. Born in Marseilles of Algerian Kabyle descent, he represented everything about the positive face of multi-ethnic France. In 1998 he was playing for Juventus FC.

France topped their group with relative ease, beating South Africa, Saudi Arabia and Denmark. They were forced into extra time to beat Paraguay. The quarter-finals against Italy went to penalties.

The semi-final was against the tournament's outsiders, Croatia, who went 1-0 up in the first minute of the second half. France won 2-1 to go on to meet Brazil in the final.

"We were 23 guys representing France, an entire country. And we were lucky we were able to do that in our own country.

"What I take with me about this victory – beyond winning, because winning is great – was to see all those people on the streets, the mix of all the different kinds of people on the streets, getting together and thinking of only one thing – to party.

"I still get goose bumps every time I talk about it.

"I hadn't scored in the tournament until the final. There was a lot of pressure on my shoulders. It almost sounds mean, but I said to myself, 'That's it. I got it.'

"So it was a great relief for me, because, after that, my final was completely different. I was liberated – having scored one goal, I was completely liberated.

↑ **Zidane heads to give France the lead in the 27th minute.**

"It remains the most beautiful thing that has happened to me

because you can always talk about a career, but a World Cup, winning it and scoring two goals, I don't think many players can say the same thing. So I'm proud, proud for my family above anything else as well, because they have always been there for me, believed in me, and it's important, when there is that amount of pressure, to be able to let go at one point, and give thanks to them. I was able to do that in the final.

"It was very emotional. You can see it: everyone was happy, some were crying, some were laughing. For my part, both in victory and in defeat, I tend to keep more to myself.

"You can see I was happy, but my strongest feelings were when I went up to the stands, when we got the Cup, and then when we went back down, I saw my wife and Enzo, who is my eldest son, in her arms; he was three at the time. The fact that he could see me and that I could see him crying, that's when my feelings got to me because he was the most beautiful thing I had and to see him cry, it was very emotional.

"My greatest emotion was to see my son cry and take him in my arms."

A million people of every background and ethnicity piled into the Champs Elysées to celebrate the FIFA World Cup™ win. The country was able to celebrate a new kind of unity in light of the victory.

In 2001 Zidane went to play for the star-studded Real Madrid for a record fee of EUR 77.5 million. In his first season he scored the greatest goal in Champions League history to win the trophy. He was named FIFA World Player of the Year three times. He retired from playing in 2006 and is now manager at Real Madrid. He still plays many charity football matches and has been a United Nations goodwill ambassador since 2001.

Zidane also scored a penalty in the 2006 FIFA World Cup™ Final, his last match for France.

1998

Emmanuel
PETIT

TEAM   France

BORN   22 September 1970

THE MATCH   In 1998 the FIFA World Cup was
hosted by France. The final was
played on 12 July in the Stade de
France, Paris.

ATTENDANCE   80,000

France 3–0 Brazil

THE GOAL   Petit scored France's third goal in
the 90th minute.

PHOTOGRAPH   Petit at the Stade de France, Paris

Although France had the advantage of being hosts, the team's prospects did not look good. Petit had been signed to AS Monaco FC by then manager Arsène Wenger at the age of 18. In 1997 he followed Wenger to Arsenal. Weeks before setting off for the FIFA World Cup™ Finals Petit had won the Premier League and FA Cup with his new team.

"Before the tournament no one in France thought we had a chance. I think it made us stronger."

France made a convincing start, beating South Africa 3-0, Saudi Arabia 4-0 and Denmark 2-1. In the quarter-final Italy took them to penalties and they beat Croatia 2-1 to get to the final.

"We were staying at Clairefontaine [the French national football training centre] where we always stay. I had been staying in the same room for 13 years so it was like home. While we were there it was very normal, very peaceful, but as soon as we left to go to the Stade de France – it's a one-hour drive – everybody was clamouring to see us, arriving by motorcycle, in cars ... People were sleeping on the roadside and they were all shouting out at us ... It was amazing.

"Yeah, we arrived probably three hours before kick-off, far too early, and it's like we all became machines. Everybody knew what to do – the preparation, mental, physical, where you change, where you go to get a massage, the way to try to compose yourself, to focus on the game, try to avoid everything negative. It's like you're above it. You've been made to play and win that game.

"With no disrespect, we weren't afraid of Brazil. The way we were playing I'm not sure anyone could have beaten us. We had scored 13 goals, divided among eight players. That's a team. Normally you rely on one or two to score goals.

"I like to take my time, no rush. When I see the opposition, I never look at them. The main opponent for me is myself. If I'm confident, if I'm OK, I don't care who I'm playing against. I go [*whistles to himself*], always focused, straight, look straight, never look around, focus … like a machine.

↘ **Petit is challenged by Cafu before going on to score France's third goal.**

"When you are a footballer, it [the World Cup] is like the Holy Grail.

When I was a kid I was training to be a professional footballer but winning the World Cup …? It's not a dream, it's more than that, it's almost impossible. Winning the World Cup is incredible, but to win and score? You couldn't do that in ten lifetimes.

"I scored in the final of the World Cup, but winning the World Cup was the best. Scoring in a World Cup Final was the strawberry on the cake, but the most important thing was winning the World Cup.

"It's just football – football with 22 men on the pitch – but it's like a religion. People will die for that. It's nonsense, but that's the way it is.

"I always took corners and free kicks. I could see the Brazilians would always focus on the tallest player in the box. The tallest isn't always the best header of the ball. At the first post there were always one Brazilian player and second [player] probably two metres behind so there was space for somebody to come in, who can come very fast and jump in with the right timing. I hit it fast and just high enough to clear the head of the first guy. Zidane was right there and he headed the goal. And then just just before half-time he did it again.

At half-time Aimé Jacquet [France manager 1993-8] had to tell us to calm down. We were so excited but he was right – even at 2-0 anything can happen. Brazil put a lot of pressure on us. They hit the post and [Fabien] Barthez had to make two brilliant saves.

"I was probably seven, eight years old, and usually you forget your dreams in the morning, but this one stayed with me. A few years before 1998 I did an interview and I said that, when I was a kid, I'd had a dream. I dreamed that France was hosting the World Cup and that France played in the final against Brazil and they won 2-0. So it was quite a surprise to me that in 1998 we hosted the World Cup and I had the chance to play in the final. A few minutes before the end I looked at Frank Leboeuf; I was playing as a central defender because of the sending-off of Marcel Desailly, and I said to Frank, 'My dream is coming true, we're going to win 2-0.' And then a few minutes later I scored the third goal, so I wrecked my dream. But I'm OK with that.

"When Patrick [Viera] gave me the ball I had space enough. I knew that I was ahead of Cafu and Dunga and there was enough space to look towards Taffarel. I could see the way he came out he didn't block his left side properly, so I could either dribble round him or lift the ball over. I decided to strike the ball straight. One shot and that's it.

↑ Petit scores France's third goal in the closing minutes of the match.

"I remember I ran like a crazy horse over there and fell like a piece of dirt on the grass somewhere.

The only thing I remember is Patrick joining me and we were like ... it was unbelievable, the noise! It was unbelievable because we had won the World Cup ... at home ... beautiful!

"It was cataclysmic; it was like a big earthquake. An amazing thing because, at that time, I don't know if you remember but there was a lot of problems in France, with immigration. A lot of fighting in the suburbs around Paris, so when we won the World Cup it was like everybody was on the same wavelength. Who cares if you're black, Algerian, white, yellow, whatever? Everybody was happy from the richest to the poorest, everybody was speaking the same language. Just because of a football match. Afterwards you saw crowds on the Champs Elysées, one million people – that hadn't happened since the Liberation.

"I had just won the double with Arsenal – the League and the FA Cup – and there was a huge celebration in Highbury. There were thousands of people in the streets wearing Arsenal shirts. So to go from that to winning and scoring in the World Cup Final ... let's just say 1998, for wine, was a very good year."

A month after the final, having won the FA Cup, the Premier League and the FIFA World Cup™, Petit put a franc in a slot machine in a hotel in Monte Carlo and won GBP 17,000. He gave it to charity. Petit played in France's attempt to defend the FIFA World Cup™ in 2002, which saw them exit the tournament at the group stage without having scored a goal. After Arsenal, he had stints at FC Barcelona and Chelsea before retiring in 2005, citing a niggling knee injury as the main reason.

Petit now lives in France where he is a TV sports analyst and an ambassador for the Homeless World Cup movement.

2002

RONALDO
Luís Nazário de Lima

TEAM	**Brazil**
BORN	**18 September 1976**
THE MATCH	**In 2002 the FIFA World Cup™ was hosted by South Korea and Japan. The final was played on 30 June in the International Stadium Yokohama.**
ATTENDANCE	**69,029**
RESULT	**Brazil 2-0 Germany**
THE GOAL	**Ronaldo scored both Brazil's goals, in the 67th and 79th minutes.**
PHOTOGRAPHED	**at Corinthians FC, São Paulo**

There had been much controversy surrounding Ronaldo's 1998 FIFA World Cup™ Final appearance when he was taken off the team sheet just before the match and then put back onto it, due to apparently having convulsive fits. He was clearly not on form and Brazil lost the final to France. By 2002 he was back. If 1986 was Maradona's World Cup, 2002 was Ronaldo's.

Brazil stormed through the group stages, scoring eleven goals in three matches, four of them Ronaldo's. They then beat Belgium, England and Turkey to meet Germany in the final. Ronaldo was at the height of his powers.

"My parents were always very strict about my studies, so football was always more like a hobby. But when I was 12 years old I started taking it very seriously. I started to get bad grades in school, so eventually I dropped the studies to dedicate myself to football. I played a lot of indoor football, where you have to carry the ball very close to your feet. Learning that helped me a lot.

"I always received a lot of support. My parents were at every game I played. Deep inside I always appreciate the support that my family gave me, because you never know when you are a child that you will become a real football player.

"I remember the '82 World Cup really well. I was six years old. The next World Cup was the same and in the next one, too. We kept losing. We did it in '86 and in '90. I always have that memory, right up until '94, and then I was in the World Cup. As children we had a lot to cry about.

"I am very proud and honoured to have been part of the Brazilian team.

It's like serving in the army of your country in a war.

↓ **Ronaldo puts the ball past German goalkeeper Oliver Kahn.**

Playing for the Brazilian squad represents playing for my people. ... A World Cup is different from any other competition. For you to be able to play for your country is something.

"World Cup football, moreover, is not like mathematics where the numbers add up and things are obvious. We live in a world where we never cease being surprised by the results. In a World Cup it's the same thing: you see the favourite teams playing incredibly and yet end up losing.

"That's maybe why so many people fall in love with this game.

"The journey to the stadium was bad. The traffic in Tokyo was very bad and we got stuck for about an hour and a half. We were really worried we would be late. We made it, but it made us very anxious.

"During the World Cup, in training, our coach Scolari [Luiz Felipe Scolari, Brazil manager 2001-2 and 2012-14] had a very big pet hatred of the frequency with which strikers waited for the rebound from the goalkeeper. He was afraid that going after the rebound could injure a player. I did it anyway and he would give me a hard time every time. And there he was, punished in the final with a goal scored in exactly that way. I had received the ball and then missed. I ran after the defender and pulled back, played it to Rivaldo, expecting him to perform a one-two, but he kicked it in direction of the goal. I ran, hoping that [Oliver] Kahn [the German goalkeeper] would parry the ball, and I was there and I just pushed the ball inside the net.

"The second goal was more polished.

It was a counter-attack coming from the right with [José] Kléberson, who rolled the ball through the middlefield. Rivaldo heard me screaming to open his legs and I just had the tranquillity to master the perfect control and kicked right in the corner so that Kahn could not reach.

"The feeling is unexplainable. It's really the pinnacle. It is the ultimate sense of satisfaction, pride and accomplishment.

You win a World Cup, scoring two goals, and, with all the problems I'd had months before, returning from a serious injury, to me it was really a very important time.

↑ **Ronaldo scores his second goal of the final.**

Ronaldo won the Golden Boot for the most goals scored in the 2002 finals. In that year he joined Real Madrid CF's galácticos alongside Zidane and David Beckham. His jersey sales broke all records on day one.

In 98 matches for Brazil he scored 62 goals. He won the FIFA World Player of the Year three times and the Ballon d'Or twice. He finished his career in 2011 while at Corinthians FC in São Paulo, where he still lives.

2006

Marco
MATERAZZI

TEAM	**Italy**
BORN	**19 August 1973**
THE MATCH	**In 2006 the FIFA World Cup™ was hosted by Germany. The final was played on 9 July in the Olympiastadion, Berlin.**
ATTENDANCE	**69,000**
RESULT	**Italy 1-1 France; Italy won 5-3 on penalties**
THE GOAL	**Materazzi scored in the 19th minute.**
PHOTOGRAPHED	**at Stadio Giuseppe Meazza ("San Siro"), Milan**

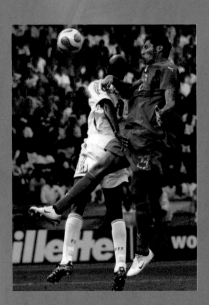

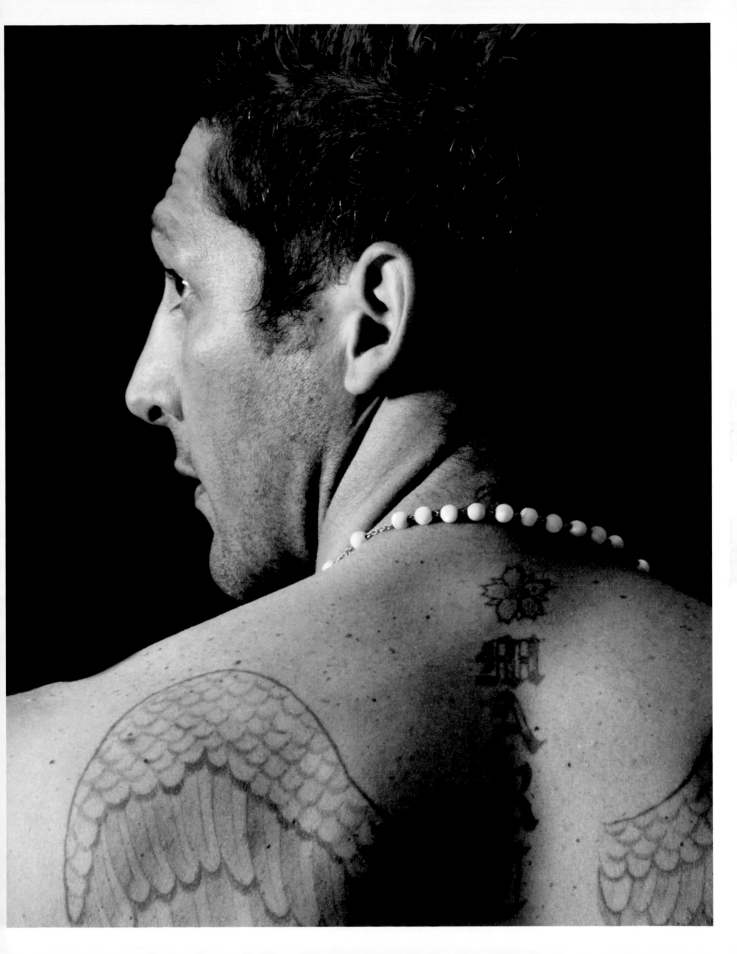

Materazzi went to the finals as a substitute and played only once in the group stages when Alessandro Nesta was injured against Croatia. In the knockout stage he started against Australia but got sent off early in the second half. Italy went through with an injury-time penalty. Materazzi missed the quarter-final through suspension but played the whole of the semi-final against Germany.

"My dad was a professional footballer, so there was always a ball and boots around. The football boots were polished with seal fat, like in the olden days, with that unusual and unmistakeable smell – these are things I remember most from when I was a boy. My dad used to move around, so my mum made sacrifices for us. We always went to school, although it's best not to talk about how I did at school.

"My siblings ... when there was a World Cup, they would make fun of me, especially my sister. She would say, 'When are you going?' I'd say, 'You'll see, you'll see, next year, next World Cup, I'll be there too.' Seeing no prospects for me, they'd say, 'Look, Marco, another World Cup has come round – when are *you* going?' Every time, I would say, 'You'll see, in four years' time I'll be going, in four years' time.' Then in the end I went for real.

"I was still an amateur at 22.

"To win the World Cup, you need a touch of good luck and I think within the group there was real conviction.

"So as not to tempt fate we said things like 'Where are we going?' – 'We're going straight home. Let's hope to get through the first round.' But in the end there was this great conviction and we showed it game by game.

"They were all single rooms – I had an adjoining room to [Alberto] Gilardino's – but we were always all together; five or six in each room, because we wanted to be with one other. Some would be playing on the PlayStation, others would be playing cards, others on the computer. They were all single rooms, but not single because we were always all together. They are the nicest memories I have of the World Cup.

"I won't say my room was the room of the goal scorers but we were lucky. There was [Fabio] Grosso, there was [Vincenzo] Iaquinta, there was Gilardino, and there was me. We all scored in that World Cup. In fact, before the final, the four of us made a pact that whoever scored in the final would give a present to the other three. I scored a goal and I gave them all a present.

"The black and gold balls were only for the finals, so we all took one from training and had each other sign them. For our final training session there were none left so we had to train with the other ones that weren't the World Cup balls.

"We bought a ghetto blaster and we used to play it at full volume. And someone would be DJ and all the others would shout requests. We made the whole bus shake. I said, 'If we win the final, I'll get off the bus with the music blaring. All the journalists thought I didn't want to talk but it was because I'd made the bet.'

"We'd seen France do their final training session and they were truly big, tall, strong and skilful. They were impressive, so we needed to get some good rest. When

↓ **Materazzi heads to equalise for Italy in the 19th minute.**

we arrived at the stadium, there were so many people that it almost didn't seem real. Usually, when you arrive at the stadium, there's only a few people – I mean, when you go to see the pitch. Instead, it was already almost full.

"There was a lot of tension but I was laughing and joking because it was a football game; it wasn't a war.'

"I gave away a penalty and I was thinking, 'Oh, no, this just isn't my game.'

"Then instead at the 19th minute, when the corner came in, Fabio Cannavaro [Italy captain] had said to me to go early. And I did. In fact, he was the first one who came up to me. He turned me round and said, 'I told you so.'

"After the goal I screamed, 'Mamma, it's yours',

if I remember well. Because in that moment that's what I thought and my heart made me think.

"Daniela, my wife, told me later that she hadn't realised who had scored, and when [Gennaro] Gattuso's wife told her – 'Look, Marco scored' – for a split second she saw a ray of light cross the stadium.

"For me, that World Cup was a kind of retribution. My first World Cup hadn't gone well and I was criticised again [for my record] in the Euros so when I took Nesta's place I was at a crossroads. If it didn't go well ... well, I don't know what would have happened.

"In the penalties, I went second. With every goal we scored I cried with joy and with every goal of theirs I suffered. But then in the end we won and that's what counts.

"I think climbing those steps with the music from the film *Gladiator* playing – I don't think there is anything to equal it, because you feel like the strongest man on earth, me and my team-mates and all the staff, and that was the best evening, I think.

"I heard rumours from FIFA about me needing to be brought to justice [for the altercation with Zidane] rather than someone else. I was labelled as the provoker – the only player in history to receive a two-match ban for teasing!

The 2002 final is remembered for Zidane's head-butting offence against Materazzi and for his subsequently being sent off as much as for anything else. Neither Materazzi nor Zidane have ever disclosed the comment that provoked the head butt.

Materazzi stayed at Inter Milan until 2011. In 2014 he became manager of Chennaiyin FC in the Indian Super League, leaving in 2016.

Zinedine
ZIDANE

TEAM: France

BORN: 23 June 1972

THE MATCH: In 2006 the FIFA World Cup™ was hosted by Germany. The final was played on 9 July 2006 in the Olympiastadion, Berlin

ATTENDANCE: 69,000

RESULT: Italy 1-1 France. Italy won 5-3 on penalties

THE GOAL: Zidane scored a penalty in the 7th minute.

PHOTOGRAPHED: in Manchester

Zidane had taken France to victory in the 1998 final and played a minimal role in France's disastrous 2002 finals, missing the first two matches through injury and clearly not on form for their final group game against Denmark. France crashed out of the tournament without scoring a goal.

In 2006 France scraped out of the group stage behind Switzerland having beaten Togo, and drawn against Switzerland and South Korea. In the first knockout stage they beat Spain 3-1, with Zidane scoring in injury time. Zidane was the man of the match in their victory against Brazil and he scored the only goal in the semi-final against Portugal to take them to the final.

The final is remembered for two instances: the confidence of Zidane's penalty in the seventh minute, and his head butting of Materazzi during extra time, and subsequent sending off. France lost on penalties and Zidane never kicked a ball for France again.

see also pages 172-5

SOUTH
AFRICA
2010

FIFA
WORLD CUP

Andrés
INIESTA

TEAM	**Spain**
BORN	**11 May 1984**
THE MATCH	**In 2010 the FIFA World Cup™ was hosted by South Africa. The final was played on 11 July at Soccer City, Johannesburg.**
ATTENDANCE	**84,490**
RESULT	**Spain 1-0 Netherlands**
THE GOAL	**Iniesta scored in the 116th minute.**
PHOTOGRAPHED	**at FC Barcelona**

niesta came up through the youth academy at FC Barcelona, making his first-team debut at 18. The Barcelona team in 2009 had just won the Spanish treble (La Liga, Copa del Rey, and the UEFA Champions League, and seven members of the team we're included in the Spanish team that travelled to South Africa. Although Spain had no real previous form in World Cups, the success of FC Barcelona and their contribution to the Spanish team meant that expectations were high.

"Spain had never really achieved anything. It's hard though because in a World Cup there are a lot of factors. It is not only the technique or the talent that count. There are a lot of factors that make you go home or stay. In 2010 a set of the right conditions came together for us after many years of work. I always believed we could do it.

"We had a very positive mentality, but we knew it was going to be very difficult. Strangely, what was really important was how we reacted to losing to Switzerland in our first match. it was very important to keep calm and keep believing. That really made a difference.

"The last group game against Chile was a turning point, too. We had to win that or we were out because we'd lost to Switzerland. Winning that really helped our confidence, and mine, too, because I'd scored the winner. After that I think we thought we could win the World Cup.

"The aim was always to go as far as possible so when we got to the semi-final that seemed huge and then we beat Germany, one of the best teams.

So we thought, let's not stop here. Let's win the World Cup.

"It might be hard to understand but the preparation for the World Cup Final is the same as the preparation for any other match. It was very normal. You wake up, have breakfast, have lunch, take a nap, play the match. It really is as simple as that.

"You could hear the noise in the tunnel, but it was odd in that, because of the vuvuzelas, everybody was making the same noise. It wasn't Spanish or Dutch; it was just one big noise. In the tunnel I don't look at anyone. I was just thinking my own thing, just wanting to be on the pitch, not wanting to be in the tunnel.

"Standing for the National Anthems is special. It is a dream coming true."

The match was a brutal affair with a total of 14 yellow cards being handed out by the English referee Howard Webb as he tried to keep the match under control. The main offenders were the Dutch, who seemed intent on winning by brute force.

"The first half was neck and neck. It was very hard for us to find our formula. We changed things at half-time and decided to hold onto the ball more. We came out more sure of ourselves. I thought we would do it in 90 minutes, but when it went to extra time

I was convinced we were going to score at any moment, that we were going to do it.

"In the second half of extra time it is impossible not to think about penalties. The match was coming to an end.

"I remember all the play from our goal line until the ball reached my feet. When Cesc [Fàbregas] passed me the ball, well, it was madness. It is very difficult for me to express what I felt at that moment because it was the maximum; you know, it is extra time, it is scoring the winning goal in the World Cup Final. It's hard to describe. It's very, very special.

"There were only a few minutes left but it seemed longer. All you want is to hear the final whistle. And then you hear it and everyone is running, laughing, crying. The first thing that comes to your mind is your family, your girlfriend, your people, the difficult moments you have been through to overcome things to get to that moment.

"In my case, I also thought of Dani Jarque [Spanish footballer and captain of RCD Espanyol who died of a heart attack in 2009, aged 26]. He was a friend of mine and I dedicated that very special goal to him."

On scoring his goal, Iniesta took off his shirt revealing a T-shirt that read "Dani Jarque siempre con nosotros" ("Dani Jarque, always with us") in tribute to his close friend.

↓ **Iniesta scores the only goal of the final to give Spain victory.**

Iniesta was named Man of the Match for the 2010 FIFA World Cup™ Final. Spain won the European Championship for the second time in a row in 2012. Iniesta was Man of the Match in the final and voted Player of the Tournament. He has been voted into the UEFA Team of the Year six times and he has been voted into the FIFA World XI on eight occasions. He won the UEFA Best Player in Europe award in 2012 and was named the IFFHS World's Best Playmaker in 2012 and 2013. He is captain of FC Barcelona.

FIFA WORLD CUP
Brasil

© FIFA TM

Mario
GÖTZE

TEAM	**Germany**
BORN	**3 June 1992**
THE MATCH	**In 2014 the FIFA World Cup™ was hosted by Brazil. The final was played on 13 July in the Estádio de Maracanã, Rio de Janeiro.**
ATTENDANCE	**74,738**
RESULT	**Germany 1-0 Argentina**
THE GOAL	**Götze scored in the 113th minute.**
PHOTOGRAPHED	**during training with the national team in Dusseldorf**

Germany travelled to Brazil as one of the favourites to win the tournament. They met Argentina in the final for the third time.

In 2014 Götze was playing at FC Bayern Munich, having previously been at Borussia Dortmund from 2009 to 2013. His transfer fee of EUR 37 million, a German record at the time, did not guarantee him a place in the starting line-up in Brazil. He played 90 minutes in the opening game against Portugal, but he would not play 90 minutes again. Against Ghana he was taken off after 69 minutes; against Algeria he was taken off after 46 minutes. He played only the last seven minutes in the quarter-final against France and he was not even on the bench for the 7-1 semi-final routing of Brazil. In the final he came on in the 88th minute.

↓ Götze scores the winning goal for Germany.

"I didn't expect to play in the semi-final. The day before we had the training session, you can normally tell then what the line-up will be like the following day. Somehow I just enjoyed watching the match. Of course, at that point I didn't have a choice, although you like to participate of course.

"On the one hand you're happy to be in the final, to have come this far with the team and everything around it, but on the other hand you're a bit disappointed, of course, not to be out on the pitch, but I think that's normal. Everyone who's there wants to play and wants to perform, wants to score goals and wants to help the team. Basically, you want to be on the pitch. However, somehow I knew that I'd definitely play, that I'd definitely get minutes on the pitch.

"When we got to Brazil everything was very good. All the arrangements, everything was taken care of, we all got on very well. Everyone fought for their place ... Of course everyone wanted to play. That's part of it. A certain rivalry has to be there because otherwise we'd probably get to a standstill at some point.

"The thing is, when the whistle blows it is still a football match. There's a lot at stake but it's 90 minutes of playing football."

It was still 0-0, with minutes to go.

"Joachim Löw [Germany manager 2006 – present] just said to me, 'Go and show the world that you're better than Messi. I know you can pull it off.'"

"I was quite relaxed. I'd been on the bench for 85 minutes. Coming on when it's 0-0 means you can do something, though. That makes a difference.

"Well, I think it was a normal situation. At the beginning we came from the left side, [André] Schürrle had the ball and started dribbling, and because of that I ran into the centre to create a bit of room for him on the left side. I ran into the centre, hoping he saw me and he just played the ball in. I controlled it with my chest, and then I struck with my left foot and it went in. You can't really practise that beforehand. You don't have time to think. It's instinctive.

You just have to be quick.

"It all happens so quickly – you get up, you cheer, team-mates come – but at that point you know that there are still a few minutes left to play. You look at the clock straight away – how much longer? – and you know it could still happen that in the coming few minutes there's a goal against us, and then the score would be 1-1 and the whole thing useless. That's why it's about more than just scoring the goal, but also about getting the thing over and done with.

"They had a free kick very late on. We knew it was their last chance. There were three of us in the wall and we were just hoping nothing happened. The three of us were standing there thinking, 'Please don't go in, please don't, please don't.' And then it didn't. It was really cool.

"At the final whistle it was just pure relief. We had been under so much pressure. We had worked so hard. You think of your family. My girlfriend was there. My father was there. You feel like you want to say thank you to all the people who helped you get there, who supported you.

↑ **Götze savours FIFA World Cup™ Final victory.**

Götze returned to Borussia Dortmund in 2016.
    He has recently been diagnosed with myopathy, a muscle disorder that may explain his
loss of form in recent years.

1930

URUGUAY

DATES: 13TH–30TH JULY

COUNTRIES COMPETING: 13 TEAMS

TOP SCORER: GUILLERMO STÁBILE – 8 GOALS

The inaugural FIFA World Cup™ was held in Uruguay, the Olympic champions and a country celebrating its centenary of its first constitution. The 13 teams competed in four groups with the winner progressing to the semi-finals.

FIRST ROUND

GROUP 1

TEAM	PLD	W	D	L	GF	GA	GD	PTS
Argentina	3	3	0	0	10	4	+6	6
Chile	3	2	0	1	5	3	+2	4
France	3	1	0	2	4	3	+1	2
Mexico	3	0	0	3	4	13	-9	0

GROUP 2

TEAM	PLD	W	D	L	GF	GA	GD	PTS
Yugoslavia	2	2	0	0	6	1	+5	4
Brazil	2	1	0	1	5	2	+3	2
Bolivia	2	0	0	2	0	8	-8	0

GROUP 3

TEAM	PLD	W	D	L	GF	GA	GD	PTS
Uruguay	2	2	0	0	5	0	+5	4
Romania	2	1	0	1	3	5	-2	2
Peru	2	0	0	2	1	4	-3	0

GROUP 4

TEAM	PLD	W	D	L	GF	GA	GD	PTS
United States	2	2	0	0	6	0	+6	4
Paraguay	2	1	0	1	1	3	-2	2
Belgium	2	0	0	2	0	4	-4	0

Semi-finals: Uruguay 6-1 Yugoslavia • Argentina 6-1 United States

FINAL

30th July – 14.15
Attendance – 68,346
Estadio Centenario (Montevideo)

URUGUAY 4-2 ARGENTINA
Pablo Dorado (URU) 12', Carlos Peucelle (ARG) 20', Giullermo Stábile (ARG) 37', Pedro Cea (URU) 57', Victoriano Iriarte (URU) 68', Héctor Castro (URU) 89'.

1934

ITALY

27TH MAY–10TH JUNE

COUNTRIES COMPETING: 16 TEAMS

TOP SCORER: OLDŘICH NEJEDLÝ (CZECHOSLOVAKIA) – 5 GOALS

Sixteen teams competed in a straight knockout tournament with 30 minutes extra time played in the event of a tie, with a rematch played the next day should the teams remain level.

First round : Italy 7-1 United States • Spain 3-1 Brazil
Austria 3-2 France (aet) • Hungary 4-2 Egypt

Czechoslovakia 2-1 Romania • Switzerland 3-2 Netherlands
Germany 5-2 Belgium • Sweden 3-2 Argentina

Quarter-finals: Italy 1-0 Spain (after the initial tie finished 1-1)
Austria 2-1 Hungary • Czechoslovakia 3-2 Switzerland
Germany 2-1 Sweden

Semi-finals: Italy 1-0 Austria • Czechoslovakia 3-1 Germany

Third place: Germany 3-2 Austria

FINAL

10th June – 17.30
Attendance – 55,000
Stadio Nazionale PNF (Rome)

ITALY 2-1 CZECHOSLOVAKIA (AET)
Antonín Puč (TCH) 71', Raimundo Orsi (ITA) 81', Angelo Schiavio (ITA) 95'

1938

FRANCE

4TH JUNE–19TH JUNE

COUNTRIES COMPETING: 15 TEAMS

TOP SCORER: LEÔNIDAS (BRAZIL) – 7 GOALS

For the second and last time, the FIFA World Cup™ was played as a straight knockout tournament, with Sweden getting a bye in the First round when Austria united with Germany and thus withdrew from the tournament.

First round : Italy 2-1 Norway • France 3-1 Belgium
Brazil 6-5 Poland (aet) • Czechoslovakia 3-0 Netherlands
Hungary 6-0 Dutch East Indies

Switzerland 4-2 Germany (after the initial tie finished 1-1)
Sweden (bye) — Austria (withdrew)
Cuba 2-1 Romania (after the first tie finished 3-3)

Quarter-finals: Italy 3-1 France
Brazil 2-1 Czechoslovakia (after the initial tie finished 1-1)
Hungary 2-0 Switzerland • Sweden 8-0 Cuba

Semi-finals: Italy 2-1 Brazil • Hungary 5-1 Sweden

Third place: Brazil 4-2 Sweden

FINAL

19th June – 17.00
Attendance – 45,000
Stade Olympique de Colombes (Paris)

ITALY 4—2 HUNGARY
Gino Colaussi (ITA) 6', Pál Titkos (HUN) 8', Silvio Piola (ITA) 16', Gino Colaussi (ITA) 35', György Sárosi (HUN) 70', Silvio Piola (ITA) 82'

1950

BRAZIL

24TH JUNE–16TH JULY

COUNTRIES COMPETING: 13 TEAMS

TOP SCORER: ADEMIR (BRAZIL) – 8 GOALS

The first round comprised four groups (or "pools") of four teams with the top team in each group advancing to the final group stage to determine the winner. Owing to the withdrawal of two teams, Group 3 consisted of only 3 teams and Group 4 of only two teams.

FIRST ROUND

GROUP 1

TEAM	PLD	W	D	L	GF	GA	GD	PTS
Brazil	3	2	1	0	8	2	+6	5
Yugoslavia	3	2	0	1	7	3	+4	4
Switzerland	3	1	1	1	4	6	-2	3
Mexico	3	0	0	3	2	10	-8	0

GROUP 2

TEAM	PLD	W	D	L	GF	GA	GD	PTS
Spain	3	3	0	0	6	1	+5	6
Chile	3	1	0	2	5	6	-1	2
England	3	1	0	2	2	2	0	2
USA	3	1	0	2	4	8	-4	2

GROUP 3

TEAM	PLD	W	D	L	GF	GA	GD	PTS
Sweden	2	1	0	1	5	4	+1	3
Italy	2	1	0	0	4	3	+1	2
Paraguay	2	0	0	1	2	4	-2	1
India (withdrew)	0	0	0	0	0	0	0	0

GROUP 4

TEAM	PLD	W	D	L	GF	GA	GD	PTS
Uruguay	1	1	0	0	8	0	+8	2
Bolivia	1	0	0	1	0	8	-8	0
France (withdrew)	0	0	0	0	0	0	0	0

FINAL ROUND

TEAM	PLD	W	D	L	GF	GA	GD	PTS
Uruguay	3	2	1	0	7	5	+2	5
Brazil	3	2	0	1	14	4	+10	4
Sweden	3	1	0	2	6	11	-5	2
Spain	3	0	1	2	4	11	-7	1

1954

SWITZERLAND

16TH JUNE–4TH JULY

COUNTRIES COMPETING: 16 TEAMS

TOP SCORER: SÁNDOR KOCSIS (HUNGARY) – 9 GOALS

The first round comprised four groups of four teams. Each group contained two seeded and two unseeded teams. Each seeded team played the unseeded teams in their group. The top two teams in each group progressed to the knockout stages. If the top two teams were level on points, a draw would decide which progressed. If the second and third placed teams drew on points, a play-off would decide which advanced.

FIRST ROUND

GROUP 1

TEAM	PLD	W	D	L	GF	GA	GD	PTS
Brazil	2	1	1	0	6	1	+5	3
Yugoslavia	2	1	1	0	2	1	+1	3
France	2	1	0	1	3	3	0	2
Mexico	2	0	0	2	2	8	–6	0

GROUP 2

TEAM	PLD	W	D	L	GF	GA	GD	PTS
Hungary	2	2	0	0	17	3	+14	4
Germany FR	3	2	0	1	14	11	+3	4
Turkey	3	1	0	2	10	11	–1	2
South Korea	2	0	0	2	0	16	–16	0

GROUP 3

TEAM	PLD	W	D	L	GF	GA	GD	PTS
Uruguay	2	2	0	0	9	0	+9	4
Austria	2	2	0	0	6	0	+6	4
Czechoslovakia	2	0	0	2	0	7	–7	0
Scotland	2	0	0	2	0	8	–8	0

GROUP 4

TEAM	PLD	W	D	L	GF	GA	GD	PTS
Switzerland	3	2	0	1	6	4	+2	4
England	2	1	1	0	6	4	+2	3
Italy	3	1	0	2	6	7	–1	2
Belgium	2	0	1	1	5	8	–3	1

Quarter-finals: Uruguay 4-2 England
Austria 7-5 Switzerland • Germany FR 2-0 Yugoslavia
Hungary 4-2 Brazil

Semi-finals: Germany FR 6-1 Austria
Hungary 4-2 Uruguay

Third place: Austria 3-1 Uruguay

FINAL

4th July – 17.00
Attendance – 62,500
Wankdorf Stadium (Bern)

GERMANY FR 3-2 HUNGARY

Ferenc Puskás 6', Zoltán Czibor 8', Max Morlock 10',
Helmut Rahn 18', 84'

1958

SWEDEN

8TH JUNE–29TH JUNE

COUNTRIES COMPETING: 16 TEAMS

TOP SCORER: JUST FONTAINE (FRANCE) – 13 GOALS

The first round comprised four groups of four teams with the top two in each group advancing to the knockout stages. Goal average would decide who would progress if the first two teams finished on equal points. A play-off would decide which team would go forward if two teams were in equal second place.

FIRST ROUND

GROUP 1

TEAM	PLD	W	D	L	GF	GA	GD	PTS
Northern Ireland	4	2	1	1	6	6	0	5
Germany FR	3	1	2	0	7	5	+2	4
Czechoslovakia	4	1	1	2	9	6	+3	3
Argentina	3	1	0	2	5	10	–5	2

GROUP 2

TEAM	PLD	W	D	L	GF	GA	GD	PTS
Yugoslavia	3	1	2	0	7	6	+1	4
France	3	2	0	1	11	7	+4	5
Paraguay	3	1	1	1	9	12	–3	3
Scotland	3	0	1	2	4	6	–2	1

GROUP 3

TEAM	PLD	W	D	L	GF	GA	GD	PTS
Sweden	3	2	1	0	5	1	+4	5
Wales	4	1	3	0	4	3	+1	5
Hungary	4	1	1	2	7	5	+2	3
Mexico	3	0	1	2	1	8	–7	1

GROUP 4

TEAM	PLD	W	D	L	GF	GA	GD	PTS
Brazil	3	2	1	0	5	0	+5	5
Soviet Union	4	2	1	1	5	4	+1	5
England	4	0	3	1	4	5	–1	3
Austria	3	0	1	2	2	7	–5	1

Quarter-finals: Brazil 1-0 Wales
Germany FR 1-0 Yugoslavia • Sweden 2-0 Soviet Union
France 4-0 Northern Ireland

Semi-finals: Sweden 3-1 Germany FR • Brazil 5-2 France

Third place: France 6-3 Germany FR

FINAL

29th June – 15.00
Attendance – 49,737
Råsunda Stadium (Solna)

BRAZIL 5-2 SWEDEN

Nils Liedholm 4', Vavá 9', 32', Pelé 55', 90',
Mário Zagallo 68', Agne Simonsson 80'

1962

CHILE

30TH MAY–17TH JUNE

COUNTRIES COMPETING: 16 TEAMS

TOP SCORER: FLÓRIÁN ALBERT (HUNGARY), GARRINCHA (BRAZIL), VAVÁ (BRAZIL), VALENTIN IVANOV (SOVIET UNION), DRAŽAN JERKOVIĆ (YUGOSLAVIA), LEONEL SÁNCHEZ (CHILE) – 9 GOALS

The first round comprised four groups of four teams with the top two in each group advancing to the quarter-finals.

FIRST ROUND

GROUP 1

TEAM	PLD	W	D	L	GF	GA	GD	PTS
Soviet Union	3	2	1	0	8	5	+3	5
Yugoslavia	3	2	0	1	8	3	+5	4
Uruguay	3	1	0	2	4	6	−2	2
Colombia	3	0	1	2	5	11	−6	1

GROUP 2

TEAM	PLD	W	D	L	GF	GA	GD	PTS
Germany FR	3	2	1	0	4	1	+3	5
Chile	3	2	0	1	5	3	+2	4
Italy	3	1	1	1	3	2	+1	3
Switzerland	3	0	0	3	2	8	−6	0

GROUP 3

TEAM	PLD	W	D	L	GF	GA	GD	PTS
Brazil	3	2	1	0	4	1	+3	5
Czechoslovakia	3	1	1	1	2	3	−1	3
Spain	3	1	0	2	2	3	−1	2
Mexico	3	1	0	2	3	4	−1	2

GROUP 4

TEAM	PLD	W	D	L	GF	GA	GD	PTS
Hungary	3	2	1	0	8	2	+6	5
England	3	1	1	1	4	3	+1	3
Argentina	3	1	1	1	2	3	−1	3
Bulgaria	3	0	1	2	1	7	−6	1

Quarter-finals: Chile 2-1 Soviet Union
Brazil 3-1 England • Czechoslovakia 1-0 Hungary
Yugoslavia 1-0 Germany FR

Semi-finals: Czechoslovakia 3-1 Yugoslavia
Brazil 4-2 Chile

Third place: Chile 1-0 Yugoslavia

FINAL

17th June – 14.30
Attendance – 68,679
Estadio Nacional (Santiago)

BRAZIL 3-1 CZECHOSLOVAKIA

Amarildo 17', Josef Masopust 15', Zito 69', Vavá 78'

1966

ENGLAND

11TH JULY–31ST JULY

COUNTRIES COMPETING: 16 TEAMS

TOP SCORER: EUSÉBIO (PORTUGAL) – 9 GOALS

The first round comprised four groups of four teams with the top two in each group advancing to the knockout stages.

FIRST ROUND

GROUP 1

TEAM	PLD	W	D	L	GF	GA	GD	PTS
England	3	2	1	0	4	0	+4	5
Uruguay	3	1	2	0	2	1	+1	4
Mexico	3	0	2	1	1	3	–2	2
France	3	0	1	2	2	5	–3	1

GROUP 2

TEAM	PLD	W	D	L	GF	GA	GD	PTS
Germany FR	3	2	1	0	7	1	+6	5
Argentina	3	2	1	0	4	1	+3	5
Spain	3	1	0	2	4	5	–1	2
Switzerland	3	0	0	3	1	9	–8	0

GROUP 3

TEAM	PLD	W	D	L	GF	GA	GD	PTS
Portugal	3	3	0	0	9	2	+7	6
Hungary	3	2	0	1	7	5	+2	4
Brazil	3	1	0	2	4	6	–2	2
Bulgaria	3	0	0	3	1	8	–7	0

GROUP 4

TEAM	PLD	W	D	L	GF	GA	GD	PTS
Soviet Union	3	3	0	0	6	1	+5	6
North Korea	3	1	1	1	2	4	–2	3
Italy	3	1	0	2	2	2	0	2
Chile	3	0	1	2	2	5	–3	1

Quarter-finals: England 1-0 Argentina
Germany FR 4-0 Uruguay • Soviet Union 2-1 Hungary
Portugal 5-3 North Korea

Semi-finals: Germany FR 2-1 Soviet Union
England 2-1 Portugal

Third place: Portugal 2-1 Soviet Union

FINAL

31st July – 15.00
Attendance – 96,924
Wembley Stadium (London)

ENGLAND 4-2 GERMANY FR (AET)

Helmut Haller 12', Geoff Hurst 18', 101', 120', Martin Peters 78', Wolfgang Weber 89'

1970

MEXICO

31ST MAY–21ST JUNE

COUNTRIES COMPETING: 16 TEAMS

TOP SCORER: GERD MÜLLER (GERMANY FR) – 10 GOALS

The first round comprised four groups of four teams with the top two in each group going through to the knockout stages.

FIRST ROUND

GROUP 1

TEAM	PLD	W	D	L	GF	GA	GD	PTS
Mexico	3	2	1	0	5	0	+5	5
Soviet Union	3	2	1	0	6	1	+5	5
Belgium	3	1	0	2	4	5	–1	2
El Salvador	3	0	0	3	0	9	–9	0

GROUP 2

TEAM	PLD	W	D	L	GF	GA	GD	PTS
Italy	3	1	2	0	1	0	+1	4
Uruguay	3	1	1	1	2	1	+1	3
Sweden	3	1	1	1	2	2	0	3
Israel	3	0	2	1	1	3	–2	2

GROUP 3

TEAM	PLD	W	D	L	GF	GA	GD	PTS
Brazil	3	3	0	0	8	3	+5	6
England	3	2	0	1	2	1	+1	4
Romania	3	1	0	2	4	5	–1	2
Czechoslovakia	3	0	0	3	2	7	–5	0

GROUP 4

TEAM	PLD	W	D	L	GF	GA	GD	PTS
Germany FR	3	3	0	0	10	4	+6	6
Peru	3	2	0	1	7	5	+2	4
Bulgaria	3	0	1	2	5	9	–4	4
Morocco	3	0	1	2	2	6	–4	1

Quarter-finals: Italy 4-1 Mexico
Germany FR 3-2 England (aet) • Brazil 4-2 Peru
Uruguay 1-0 Soviet Union (aet)

Semi-finals: Brazil 3-1 Uruguay
Italy 4-3 Germany FR (aet)

Third place: Germany FR 1-0 Uruguay

FINAL

21st June – 12.00
Attendance – 107,412
Estadio Azteca (Mexico City)

BRAZIL 4-1 ITALY

Pelé 18', Roberto Boninsegna 37', Gerson 66', Jairzinho 71', Carlos Alberto 86'

1974

© TM FIFA

GERMANY

13TH JUNE–7TH JULY

COUNTRIES COMPETING: 16 TEAMS

TOP SCORER: GRZEGRZ LATO (POLAND) – 7 GOALS

The first round comprised four groups of four teams with the top two in each group going through to the second round of two groups of four. The winner of each group would go through to the final. The second team in each group played each other for third place.

FIRST ROUND

GROUP 1

TEAM	PLD	W	D	L	GF	GA	GD	PTS
Germany DR	3	2	1	0	4	1	+3	5
Germany FR	3	2	0	1	4	1	+3	4
Chile	3	0	2	1	1	2	–1	2
Australia	3	0	1	2	0	5	–5	1

GROUP 2

TEAM	PLD	W	D	L	GF	GA	GD	PTS
Scotland	3	1	2	0	3	1	+2	4
Yugoslavia	3	1	2	0	10	1	+9	4
Brazil	3	1	2	0	3	0	–3	4
Zaire	3	0	0	3	0	14	–14	0

GROUP 3

TEAM	PLD	W	D	L	GF	GA	GD	PTS
Netherlands	3	2	1	0	6	1	+5	5
Sweden	3	1	2	0	3	0	+3	4
Bulgaria	3	1	2	1	2	5	–3	2
Uruguay	3	0	1	2	1	6	–5	1

GROUP 4

TEAM	PLD	W	D	L	GF	GA	GD	PTS
Poland	3	3	0	0	12	3	+9	6
Argentina	3	1	1	1	7	5	+2	3
Italy	3	1	1	1	5	4	+1	3
Haiti	3	0	0	3	2	14	–12	0

SECOND ROUND

GROUP A

TEAM	PLD	W	D	L	GF	GA	GD	PTS
Netherlands	3	3	0	0	8	0	+8	6
Brazil	3	2	0	1	3	3	0	4
Argentina	3	0	1	2	2	7	–5	1
Germany DR	3	0	1	2	1	4	–3	1

GROUP B

TEAM	PLD	W	D	L	GF	GA	GD	PTS
Germany FR	3	3	0	0	7	2	+5	6
Poland	3	2	0	1	3	2	+1	4
Sweden	3	1	0	2	4	6	–2	2
Yugoslavia	3	0	0	3	2	6	–4	0

Third place: Brazil 0-1 Poland

FINAL

7th June – 16.00
Attendance – 78,200
Olympiastadion (Munich)

NETHERLANDS 1-2 GERMANY FR

Johan Neeskens 2' (pen), Paul Breitner 25' (pen),
Gerd Müller 43'

1978

ARGENTINA

Argentina '78 © TM FIFA

1ST JUNE–25TH JULY

COUNTRIES COMPETING: 16 TEAMS

TOP SCORER: MARIO KEMPES (ARGENTINA) – 6 GOALS

The first round comprised four groups of four teams with the top two in each group going through to the second round of two groups of four. The winner of each group would go through to the final.

FIRST ROUND

GROUP 1

TEAM	PLD	W	D	L	GF	GA	GD	PTS
Italy	3	3	0	0	6	2	+4	6
Argentina	3	2	0	1	4	3	+1	4
France	3	1	0	2	5	5	0	2
Hungary	3	0	0	3	3	8	–5	0

GROUP 2

TEAM	PLD	W	D	L	GF	GA	GD	PTS
Poland	3	2	1	0	4	1	+3	5
Germany FR	3	1	2	0	6	0	+6	4
Algeria	3	1	1	1	3	2	+1	3
Mexico	3	0	0	3	2	12	–10	0

GROUP 3

TEAM	PLD	W	D	L	GF	GA	GD	PTS
Brazil	3	1	2	0	2	1	+1	4
Austria	3	2	0	1	3	2	+1	4
Spain	3	1	1	1	2	2	0	3
Sweden	3	0	1	2	1	3	–2	1

GROUP 4

TEAM	PLD	W	D	L	GF	GA	GD	PTS
Peru	3	2	1	0	7	2	+5	5
Scotland	3	2	1	1	5	6	–1	3
Netherlands	3	1	1	1	5	3	+2	3
Iran	3	0	1	2	2	8	–6	1

SECOND ROUND

GROUP A

TEAM	PLD	W	D	L	GF	GA	GD	PTS
Netherlands	3	2	1	0	9	4	+5	5
Italy	3	1	1	1	2	2	0	3
Austria	3	1	0	2	4	8	–4	2
Germany FR	3	0	2	1	4	5	–1	2

GROUP B

TEAM	PLD	W	D	L	GF	GA	GD	PTS
Argentina	3	2	1	0	8	0	+8	5
Brazil	3	2	1	0	6	1	+5	5
Poland	3	1	0	2	2	5	–3	2
Peru	3	0	0	3	0	10	–10	0

Third place: Brazil 2-1 Italy

FINAL

25th June – 20.00
Attendance – 71,483
Estadio Monumental (Buenos Aires)

NETHERLANDS 1-3 ARGENTINA (AET)

Mario Kempes 37', 104', Dick Nanninga 82',
Daniel Bertoni 115'

1982

SPAIN

13TH JUNE–11TH JULY

COUNTRIES COMPETING: 24 TEAMS

TOP SCORER: PAOLO ROSSI (ITALY) – 6 GOALS

The first round comprised six groups of four teams with the top two in each group going through to a knockout competition. The 12 remaining teams were divided into four new groups. The winner of each group progressed to the knockout stage.

FIRST ROUND

GROUP 1

TEAM	PLD	W	D	L	GF	GA	GD	PTS
Poland	3	1	2	0	5	1	+4	4
Cameroon	3	0	3	0	1	1	0	3
Italy	3	0	3	0	2	2	0	3
Peru	3	0	2	1	2	6	−4	2

GROUP 2

TEAM	PLD	W	D	L	GF	GA	GD	PTS
Austria	3	2	0	1	3	1	+2	4
Germany FR	3	2	0	1	6	3	+3	4
Algeria	3	2	0	1	5	5	0	4
Chile	3	0	0	3	3	8	−5	0

GROUP 3

TEAM	PLD	W	D	L	GF	GA	GD	PTS
Belgium	3	2	1	0	3	1	+2	5
Argentina	3	2	0	1	6	2	+4	4
Hungary	3	1	1	1	12	6	+6	3
El Salvador	3	0	0	3	1	13	−12	0

GROUP 4

TEAM	PLD	W	D	L	GF	GA	GD	PTS
England	3	3	0	0	6	1	+5	6
France	3	1	1	1	6	5	+1	3
Czechoslovakia	3	0	2	1	2	4	−2	2
Kuwait	3	0	1	2	2	6	−4	1

GROUP 5

TEAM	PLD	W	D	L	GF	GA	GD	PTS
Northern Ireland	3	1	2	0	2	1	+5	4
Spain	3	1	1	1	3	3	+3	3
Yugoslavia	3	1	1	1	2	2	−4	3
Honduras	3	0	2	1	2	3	−4	2

GROUP 6

TEAM	PLD	W	D	L	GF	GA	GD	PTS
Brazil	3	3	0	0	10	2	+8	6
Scotland	3	1	1	1	8	8	0	3
Soviet Union	3	1	1	1	6	4	+2	3
New Zealand	3	0	0	3	2	12	−10	0

2ND ROUND

GROUP 1

TEAM	PLD	W	D	L	GF	GA	GD	PTS
Poland	2	1	1	0	3	0	+3	3
Soviet Union	2	1	1	0	1	0	+1	3
Belgium	2	0	0	2	0	4	+4	0

GROUP 2

TEAM	PLD	W	D	L	GF	GA	GD	PTS
Germany FR	2	1	1	0	2	1	1	3
England	2	0	2	0	0	0	0	2
Spain	2	0	1	1	1	2	−1	1

GROUP 3

TEAM	PLD	W	D	L	GF	GA	GD	PTS
Italy	2	2	0	0	5	3	2	4
Brazil	2	1	0	1	5	4	1	2
Argentina	2	0	0	2	2	5	−3	0

GROUP 4

TEAM	PLD	W	D	L	GF	GA	GD	PTS
France	2	2	0	0	5	1	4	4
Austria	2	0	1	1	2	3	−1	1
Northern Ireland	2	0	1	1	3	6	−3	1

Semi-finals: Poland 0-2 Italy
Germany FR 3-3 France (5-4 pens)

Third place: Poland 3-2 France

FINAL

11th July – 20.00 Attendance – 90,000
Santiago Bernabéu Stadium (Madrid)

ITALY 3-1 GERMANY FR

Paolo Rossi 57', Marco Tardelli 69', Alessandro Altobelli 81',
Paul Breitner 83'

1986

MEXICO

31ST MAY–29TH JUNE

COUNTRIES COMPETING: 24 TEAMS

TOP SCORER: GARY LINEKER (ENGLAND) – 6 GOALS

The first round comprised six groups of four teams with the top two in each group and the four best runners up going through to a knockout competition.

GROUP A

TEAM	PLD	W	D	L	GF	GA	GD	PTS
Argentina	3	2	1	0	6	2	+4	5
Italy	3	1	2	0	5	4	+1	4
Bulgaria	3	0	2	1	2	4	–2	2
South Korea	3	0	1	2	4	7	–3	1

GROUP B

TEAM	PLD	W	D	L	GF	GA	GD	PTS
Mexico	3	2	1	0	4	2	+2	5
Paraguay	3	1	2	0	4	3	+1	4
Belgium	3	1	1	1	5	5	0	3
Iraq	3	0	0	3	1	4	–3	0

GROUP C

TEAM	PLD	W	D	L	GF	GA	GD	PTS
Soviet Union	3	2	1	0	9	1	+8	5
France	3	2	1	0	5	1	+4	5
Hungary	3	1	0	2	2	9	–7	2
Canada	3	0	0	3	0	5	–5	0

GROUP D

TEAM	PLD	W	D	L	GF	GA	GD	PTS
Brazil	3	3	0	0	5	0	+5	6
Spain	3	2	0	1	5	2	+3	4
Northern Ireland	3	0	1	2	2	6	–4	1
Algeria	3	0	1	2	1	5	–4	1

GROUP E

TEAM	PLD	W	D	L	GF	GA	GD	PTS
Denmark	3	3	0	0	5	0	+5	6
Germany FR	3	1	1	1	5	2	+3	4
Uruguay	3	0	2	2	2	6	–4	1
Scotland	3	0	1	2	1	5	–4	1

GROUP F

TEAM	PLD	W	D	L	GF	GA	GD	PTS
Morocco	3	1	2	0	3	1	+2	4
England	3	1	1	1	3	1	+2	3
Poland	3	1	1	1	1	3	–2	3
Portugal	3	1	0	2	2	4	–2	2

Second round: Soviet Union 3-4 Belgium (aet)
Mexico 2-0 Bulgaria • Argentina 1-0 Uruguay
Brazil 4-0 Poland • Italy 0-4 France
Morocco 0-1 Germany FR • England 3-0 Paraguay
Denmark 1-5 Spain

Quarter-finals: Brazil 1-1 France (4-5 pens)
Germany FR 0-0 Mexico (4-1 pens)
Spain 1-1 Belgium (4-5 pens) • Argentina 2-1 England

Semi-finals: France 0-2 Germany FR
Argentina 2-0 Belgium

Third place: France 4-2 Belgium (aet)

FINAL

29th June – 12.00
Attendance – 114,600
Estadio Azteca (Mexico City)

ARGENTINA 3-2 GERMANY FR

José Luis Brown 23', Jorge Valdano 55',
Karl-Heinz Rummenigge 74', Rudi Völler 80',
Jorge Burruchaga 83'

1990

ITALY

8TH JUNE–8TH JULY

COUNTRIES COMPETING: 24 TEAMS

TOP SCORER: SALVATORE SCHILLACI (ITALY) – 6 GOALS

ITALIA'90
© FIFA TM

The first round comprised six groups of four teams with the top two in each group and the four best runners up going through to a knockout competition.

GROUP A

TEAM	PLD	W	D	L	GF	GA	GD	PTS
Italy	3	3	0	0	4	0	+4	6
Czechoslovakia	3	2	0	1	6	3	+3	4
Austria	3	1	0	2	2	3	–1	2
USA	3	0	0	3	2	8	–6	0

GROUP B

TEAM	PLD	W	D	L	GF	GA	GD	PTS
Cameroon	3	2	0	1	3	5	–2	4
Romania	3	1	1	1	4	3	+1	3
Argentina	3	1	1	1	3	2	+1	3
Soviet Union	3	1	0	2	4	4	0	2

GROUP C

TEAM	PLD	W	D	L	GF	GA	GD	PTS
Brazil	3	3	0	0	4	1	+3	6
Costa Rica	3	2	0	1	3	2	+1	4
Scotland	3	1	0	2	2	3	+1	2
Sweden	3	0	0	3	3	6	–3	0

GROUP D

TEAM	PLD	W	D	L	GF	GA	GD	PTS
Germany FR	3	2	1	0	10	3	+7	5
Yugoslavia	3	2	0	1	6	5	+1	4
Colombia	3	1	1	1	3	2	+1	3
United Arab Emirates	3	0	0	3	2	11	–9	0

GROUP E

TEAM	PLD	W	D	L	GF	GA	GD	PTS
Spain	3	2	1	0	10	3	+7	5
Belgium	3	2	0	1	6	5	+1	4
Uruguay	3	1	1	1	3	2	+1	3
South Korea	3	0	0	3	2	11	–9	0

GROUP F

TEAM	PLD	W	D	L	GF	GA	GD	PTS
England	3	1	2	0	2	1	+1	4
Republic of Ireland	3	0	3	0	2	2	0	3
Netherlands	3	0	3	0	2	2	0	3
Egypt	3	0	2	1	1	2	–1	2

Second round: Cameroon 2-1 Colombia (aet)
Czechoslovakia 4-1 Costa Rica • Brazil 0-1 Argentina
Germany FR 2-1 Netherlands
Republic of Ireland 0-0 Romania (5-4 pens)
Spain 1-2 Yugoslavia (aet) • England 1-0 Belgium (aet)

Quarter-finals: Yugoslavia 0-0 Argentina (2-3 pens)
Italy 1-0 Republic of Ireland
Germany FR 1-0 Czechosvakia • England 3-2 Cameroon

Semi-finals: Italy 1-1 Argentina (3-4 pens)
Germany FR 1-1 England (4-3 pens)

Third place: Italy 2-1 England

FINAL

8th July – 20.00
Attendance – 73,603
Stadio Olimpico (Rome)

GERMANY FR 1-0 ARGENTINA

Andreas Brehme 85' (pen)

1994

USA

17TH JUNE–17TH JULY

COUNTRIES COMPETING: 24 TEAMS

TOP SCORERS: HRISTO STOICHKOV (BULGARIA) AND OLEG SALENKO (RUSSIA) – 6 GOALS

The first round comprised six groups of four teams with the top two in each group and the four best runners up going through to a knockout competition.

GROUP A

TEAM	PLD	W	D	L	GF	GA	GD	PTS
Romania	3	2	0	1	5	5	0	6
Switzerland	3	1	1	1	5	4	+1	4
USA	3	1	1	1	3	3	0	4
Colombia	3	1	0	2	4	5	–1	3

GROUP B

TEAM	PLD	W	D	L	GF	GA	GD	PTS
Brazil	3	2	1	0	6	1	+5	7
Sweden	3	1	2	0	6	4	+2	5
Russia	3	1	0	2	7	6	+1	3
Cameroon	3	0	1	2	3	11	–8	1

GROUP C

TEAM	PLD	W	D	L	GF	GA	GD	PTS
Germany	3	2	1	0	5	3	+2	7
Spain	3	1	2	0	6	4	+2	5
South Korea	3	0	2	1	4	5	–1	2
Bolivia	3	0	1	2	1	4	–3	1

GROUP D

TEAM	PLD	W	D	L	GF	GA	GD	PTS
Nigeria	3	2	0	1	6	2	+4	6
Bulgaria	3	2	0	1	6	3	+3	6
Argentina	3	2	0	1	6	3	+3	6
Greece	3	0	0	3	0	10	–10	0

GROUP E

TEAM	PLD	W	D	L	GF	GA	GD	PTS
Mexico	3	1	1	1	3	3	0	4
Republic of Ireland	3	1	1	1	2	2	0	4
Italy	3	1	1	1	2	2	0	4
Norway	3	1	1	1	1	1	0	4

GROUP F

TEAM	PLD	W	D	L	GF	GA	GD	PTS
Netherlands	3	2	0	1	4	3	+1	6
Saudi Arabia	3	2	0	1	4	3	+1	6
Belgium	3	2	0	1	2	1	–1	6
Morocco	3	0	0	3	2	5	–3	0

Second round: Germany 3-2 Belgium
Spain 3-0 Switzerland • Saudi Arabia 1-3 Sweden
Romani 3-2 Argentina
Netherlands 2-0 Republic of Ireland • Brazil 1-0 USA
Nigeria 1-2 Italy • Mexico 1-1 Bulgaria (1-3 pens)

Quarter-finals: Italy 2-1 Spain • Netherlands 2-3 Brazil
Bulgaria 2-1 Germany • Romania 2-2 Sweden (4-5 pens)

Semi-finals: Bulgaria 1-2 Italy • Sweden 0-1 Brazil

Third place: Sweden 4-0 Bulgaria

FINAL

17th July – 12:30
Attendance – 94,194
Rose Bowl (Los Angeles)

BRAZIL 0-0 ITALY (3-2 PENS)

1998

FRANCE

10TH JUNE–12TH JULY

COUNTRIES COMPETING: 32 TEAMS

TOP SCORER: DAVOR ŠUKER (CROATIA) – 6 GOALS

© FIFA TM

The first round comprised eight groups of four teams with the top two going through to a knockout competition.

GROUP A

TEAM	PLD	W	D	L	GF	GA	GD	PTS
Brazil	3	2	0	1	6	3	+3	6
Norway	3	1	2	0	5	4	+1	5
Morocco	3	1	1	1	5	5	0	4
Scotland	3	0	1	2	2	6	–4	1

GROUP B

TEAM	PLD	W	D	L	GF	GA	GD	PTS
Italy	3	2	1	0	7	3	+4	7
Chile	3	0	3	0	4	4	0	3
Austria	3	0	2	1	3	4	–1	2
Cameroon	3	0	2	1	2	5	–3	2

GROUP C

TEAM	PLD	W	D	L	GF	GA	GD	PTS
France	3	3	0	0	9	1	+8	9
Denmark	3	1	1	1	3	3	0	4
South Africa	3	0	2	1	3	6	–3	2
Saudi Arabia	3	0	1	2	2	7	–5	1

GROUP D

TEAM	PLD	W	D	L	GF	GA	GD	PTS
Nigeria	3	2	0	1	5	5	0	6
Paraguay	3	1	2	0	3	1	+2	5
Spain	3	1	1	1	8	4	+4	4
Bulgaria	3	0	1	2	1	7	–6	1

GROUP E

TEAM	PLD	W	D	L	GF	GA	GD	PTS
Netherlands	3	1	2	0	7	2	+5	5
Mexico	3	1	2	0	7	5	+2	5
Belgium	3	0	3	0	3	3	0	3
South Korea	3	0	1	2	2	9	–7	1

GROUP F

TEAM	PLD	W	D	L	GF	GA	GD	PTS
Germany	3	2	1	0	6	2	+4	7
Yugoslavia	3	2	1	0	4	2	+2	7
Iran	3	1	0	2	2	4	–2	3
USA	3	0	0	3	1	5	–4	0

GROUP G

TEAM	PLD	W	D	L	GF	GA	GD	PTS
Romania	3	2	1	0	4	2	+2	7
England	3	2	0	1	5	2	+3	6
Colombia	3	1	0	2	1	3	–2	3
Tunisia	3	0	1	2	1	4	–3	1

GROUP H

TEAM	PLD	W	D	L	GF	GA	GD	PTS
Argentina	3	3	0	0	7	0	+7	9
Croatia	3	2	0	1	4	2	+2	6
Jamaica	3	1	0	2	3	9	–6	3
Japan	3	0	0	3	1	4	–3	0

Second round: Italy 1-0 Norway • Brazil 4-1 Chile France 1-0 Paraguay (aet) • Nigeria 1-4 Denmark Germany 2-1 Mexico • Netherlands 2-1 Yugoslavia Romania 0-1 Croatia • Argentina 2-2 England (4-3 pens)

Quarter-finals: Italy 0-0 France (3-4 pens) Brazil 3-2 Denmark • Netherlands 2-1 Argentina Germany 0-3 Croatia

Semi-finals: Brazil 1-1 Netherlands (4-2 pens) France 2-1 Croatia

Third place: Netherlands 1-2 Croatia

FINAL

12th July – 21:00
Attendance – 80,000
Stade de France (Saint-Denis)

BRAZIL 0-3 FRANCE

Zinedine Zidane 27', 45 + 1', Emmanuel Petit 90 + 3'

2002

KOREA/JAPAN

31ST MAY–30TH JUNE

COUNTRIES COMPETING: 32 TEAMS

TOP SCORER: RONALDO (BRAZIL) – 8 GOALS

The first round comprised eight groups of four teams with the top two going through to a knockout competition.

GROUP A

TEAM	PLD	W	D	L	GF	GA	GD	PTS
Denmark	3	2	1	0	5	2	+3	7
Senegal	3	1	2	0	5	4	+1	5
Uruguay	3	0	2	1	4	5	−1	2
France	3	0	1	2	0	3	−3	1

GROUP B

TEAM	PLD	W	D	L	GF	GA	GD	PTS
Spain	3	3	0	0	9	4	+5	9
Paraguay	3	1	1	1	6	6	0	4
South Africa	3	1	1	1	5	5	0	4
Slovenia	3	0	0	3	2	7	−5	0

GROUP C

TEAM	PLD	W	D	L	GF	GA	GD	PTS
Brazil	3	3	0	0	11	3	+8	9
Turkey	3	1	1	1	5	3	+2	4
Costa Rica	3	1	1	1	5	6	−1	4
China PR	3	0	0	3	0	9	−9	0

GROUP D

TEAM	PLD	W	D	L	GF	GA	GD	PTS
South Korea	3	2	1	0	4	1	+3	7
USA	3	1	1	1	5	6	−1	4
Portugal	3	1	0	2	6	4	+2	3
Poland	3	1	0	2	3	7	−4	3

GROUP E

TEAM	PLD	W	D	L	GF	GA	GD	PTS
Germany	3	2	1	0	11	1	+10	7
Republic of Ireland	3	1	2	0	5	2	+3	5
Cameroon	3	1	1	1	2	3	−1	4
Saudi Arabia	3	0	0	3	0	12	−12	0

GROUP F

TEAM	PLD	W	D	L	GF	GA	GD	PTS
Sweden	3	1	2	0	4	3	+1	5
England	3	1	2	0	2	1	+1	5
Argentina	3	1	1	1	2	2	0	4
Nigeria	3	0	1	2	1	3	−2	1

GROUP G

TEAM	PLD	W	D	L	GF	GA	GD	PTS
Mexico	3	2	1	0	4	2	+2	7
Italy	3	1	1	1	4	3	+1	4
Croatia	3	1	0	2	2	3	−1	3
Ecuador	3	1	0	2	2	4	−2	3

GROUP H

TEAM	PLD	W	D	L	GF	GA	GD	PTS
Japan	3	2	1	0	5	2	+3	7
Belgium	3	1	2	0	6	5	+1	5
Russia	3	1	0	2	4	4	0	3
Tunisia	3	0	1	2	1	5	−4	1

Second round: Spain 1-1 Republic of Ireland (3-2 on pens)
Sweden 1-2 Senegal (aet) • Brazil 2-0 Belgium
Mexico 0-2 USA • Japan 0-1 Turkey
South Korea 2-1 Italy

Quarter-finals: England 1-2 Brazil • Germany 1-0 USA
Senegal 0-1 Turkey (aet)
Spain 0-0 South Korea (3-5 pens)

Semi-finals: Germany 1-0 South Korea
Brazil 1-0 Turkey

Third place: South Korea 2-3 Turkey

FINAL

30th June – 20:00
Attendance – 69,029
International Stadium (Yokohama)

GERMANY 0-2 BRAZIL
Ronaldo 67', 79'

2006

GERMANY

9TH JUNE–9TH JULY

COUNTRIES COMPETING: 32 TEAMS

TOP SCORER: MIROSLAV KLOSE (GERMANY) – 5 GOALS

The first round comprised eight groups of four teams with the top two going through to a knockout competition.

GROUP A

TEAM	PLD	W	D	L	GF	GA	GD	PTS
Germany	3	3	0	0	8	2	+6	9
Ecuador	3	2	0	1	5	3	+2	6
Poland	3	1	0	2	2	4	–2	3
Costa Rica	3	0	0	3	3	9	–6	0

GROUP B

TEAM	PLD	W	D	L	GF	GA	GD	PTS
England	3	2	1	0	5	2	+3	7
Sweden	3	1	2	0	3	2	+1	5
Paraguay	3	1	0	2	2	2	0	3
Trinidad and Tobago	3	0	1	2	0	4	–4	1

GROUP C

TEAM	PLD	W	D	L	GF	GA	GD	PTS
Argentina	3	2	1	0	8	1	+7	7
Netherlands	3	2	1	0	3	1	+2	7
Ivory Coast	3	1	0	2	5	63	–1	3
Serbia and Montenegro	3	0	0	3	2	10	–8	0

GROUP D

TEAM	PLD	W	D	L	GF	GA	GD	PTS
Portugal	3	3	0	0	5	1	+4	9
Mexico	3	1	1	1	4	3	+1	4
Angola	3	0	2	1	1	2	–1	2
Iran	3	0	1	2	2	6	–4	1

GROUP E

TEAM	PLD	W	D	L	GF	GA	GD	PTS
Italy	3	2	1	0	5	1	+4	7
Ghana	3	2	0	1	4	3	+1	6
Czech Republic	3	1	0	2	3	4	–1	3
USA	3	0	1	2	2	6	–4	1

GROUP F

TEAM	PLD	W	D	L	GF	GA	GD	PTS
Brazil	3	3	0	0	7	1	+6	9
Australia	3	1	1	1	5	5	0	4
Croatia	3	0	2	1	2	3	–1	2
Japan	3	0	1	2	2	7	–5	1

GROUP G

TEAM	PLD	W	D	L	GF	GA	GD	PTS
Switzerland	3	2	1	0	4	0	+4	7
France	3	1	2	0	3	1	+2	5
South Korea	3	1	1	1	3	4	–1	4
Togo	3	0	0	3	1	6	–5	0

GROUP H

TEAM	PLD	W	D	L	GF	GA	GD	PTS
Spain	3	3	0	0	8	1	+7	9
Ukraine	3	2	0	1	5	4	+1	6
Tunisia	3	0	1	2	3	6	–3	1
Saudi Arabia	3	0	1	2	2	7	–5	1

Second round: Germany 2-0 Sweden
Argentina 2-1 Mexico • England 1-0 Ecuador
Portugal 1-0 Netherlands • Italy 1-0 Australia
Switzerland 0-0 Ukraine (0-3 on pens)
Brazil 3-0 Ghana • Spain 1-3 France

Quarter-finals: Germany 1-1 Argentina (4-2 on pens)
Italy 3-0 Ukraine • England 0-0 Portugal (1-3 on pens)
Brazil 0-1 France

Semi-finals: Germany 0-2 Italy (aet)
Portugal 0-1 France

Third place: Germany 3-1 Portugal

FINAL

9th July – 20:00
Attendance – 69,000
Olympiastadion (Berlin)

ITALY 1-1 FRANCE (5-3 ON PENS)

Marco Materazzi 19', Zinedine Zidane 7'

2010

SOUTH AFRICA

11TH JUNE–11TH JULY

COUNTRIES COMPETING: 32 TEAMS

TOP SCORER: THOMAS MÜLLER (GERMANY) – 5 GOALS

The first round comprised eight groups of four teams with the top two going through to a knockout competition.

GROUP A

TEAM	PLD	W	D	L	GF	GA	GD	PTS
Uruguay	3	2	1	0	4	0	+4	7
Mexico	3	1	1	1	3	2	+1	4
South Africa	3	1	1	1	3	5	−2	4
France	3	0	1	2	1	4	−3	1

GROUP B

TEAM	PLD	W	D	L	GF	GA	GD	PTS
Argentina	3	3	0	0	7	1	+6	9
South Korea	3	1	1	1	5	6	−1	4
Greece	3	1	0	2	2	5	−3	3
Nigeria	3	0	1	2	3	5	−2	1

GROUP C

TEAM	PLD	W	D	L	GF	GA	GD	PTS
USA	3	1	2	0	4	3	+1	5
England	3	1	2	0	2	1	+1	5
Slovenia	3	1	1	1	3	3	0	4
Algeria	3	0	1	2	0	2	−2	1

GROUP D

TEAM	PLD	W	D	L	GF	GA	GD	PTS
Germany	3	2	0	1	5	1	+4	6
Ghana	3	1	1	1	2	2	0	4
Australia	3	1	1	1	3	6	+3	4
Serbia	3	1	0	2	2	3	−1	3

GROUP E

TEAM	PLD	W	D	L	GF	GA	GD	PTS
Netherlands	3	3	0	0	5	1	+4	9
Japan	3	2	0	1	4	2	+2	6
Denmark	3	1	0	2	3	6	−3	3
Cameroon	3	0	0	3	2	5	−3	0

GROUP F

TEAM	PLD	W	D	L	GF	GA	GD	PTS
Paraguay	3	1	2	0	3	1	+2	5
Slovakia	3	1	1	1	4	5	−1	4
New Zealand	3	0	3	0	2	2	0	3
Italy	3	0	2	1	4	5	−1	2

GROUP G

TEAM	PLD	W	D	L	GF	GA	GD	PTS
Brazil	3	2	1	0	5	2	+3	7
Portugal	3	1	2	0	7	0	+7	5
Ivory Coast	3	1	1	1	4	3	+1	4
North Korea	3	0	0	3	1	12	−11	0

GROUP H

TEAM	PLD	W	D	L	GF	GA	GD	PTS
Spain	3	2	0	1	4	2	+2	6
Chile	3	2	0	1	3	2	+1	6
Switzerland	3	1	1	1	1	1	0	4
Honduras	3	0	1	2	0	3	−3	1

Second round: Uruguay 2-1 South Korea
USA 1-2 Ghana (aet) • Germany 4-1 England
Argentina 3-1 Mexico • Netherlands 2-1 Slovakia
Brazil 3-0 Chile • Paraguay 0-0 Japan (5-3 on pens)
Spain 1-0 Portugal

Quarter-finals: Netherlands 2-1 Brazil
Uruguay 1-1 Ghana (4-2 on pens)
Argentina 0-4 Germany • Paraguay 0-1 Spain

Semi-finals: Uruguay 2-3 Netherlands • Germany 0-1 Spain

Third place: Uruguay 2-3 Germany

FINAL

11th July – 20:30
Attendance – 84,490
Soccer City Stadium (Johannesburg)

NETHERLANDS 0-1 SPAIN (AET)

Andrés Iniesta 116'

2014

BRAZIL

12 JUNE–13TH JULY 2014

COUNTRIES COMPETING: 32 TEAMS

TOP SCORER: JAMES RODERIGUEZ (CHILE) – 6 GOALS

The format was the same as South Africa four years prior with 32 teams competing the first round of eight groups from which the top two progressed.

GROUP A

TEAM	PLD	W	D	L	GF	GA	GD	PTS
Brazil	3	2	1	0	7	2	+5	7
Mexico	3	2	1	0	4	1	+3	7
Croatia	3	1	0	2	6	6	0	3
Cameroon	3	0	0	3	1	9	-8	0

GROUP B

TEAM	PLD	W	D	L	GF	GA	GD	PTS
Netherlands	3	3	0	0	10	3	+7	9
Chile	3	2	0	1	5	3	+2	6
Spain	3	1	0	2	4	7	-3	3
Australia	3	0	0	3	3	9	-6	0

GROUP C

TEAM	PLD	W	D	L	GF	GA	GD	PTS
Colombia	3	3	0	0	9	2	+7	9
Greece	3	1	1	1	2	4	-2	4
Ivory Coast	3	1	0	2	4	5	-1	3
Japan	3	0	1	2	2	6	-4	1

GROUP D

TEAM	PLD	W	D	L	GF	GA	GD	PTS
Costa Rica	3	2	1	0	4	1	+3	7
Uruguay	3	2	0	1	4	4	0	6
Italy	3	1	0	2	2	3	-1	3
England	3	0	1	2	2	4	-2	1

GROUP E

TEAM	PLD	W	D	L	GF	GA	GD	PTS
France	3	2	1	0	8	2	+6	7
Switzerland	3	2	0	1	7	6	+1	6
Ecuador	3	1	1	1	3	3	0	4
Honduras	3	0	0	3	1	8	-7	0

GROUP F

TEAM	PLD	W	D	L	GF	GA	GD	PTS
Argentina	3	3	0	0	6	3	+3	9
Nigeria	3	1	1	1	3	3	0	4
Bosnia and Herzegovina	3	1	0	2	4	4	0	3
Iran	3	0	1	2	1	4	-3	1

GROUP G

TEAM	PLD	W	D	L	GF	GA	GD	PTS
Germany	3	2	1	0	7	2	+5	7
United States	3	1	1	1	4	4	0	4
Portugal	3	1	1	1	4	7	-3	4
Ghana	3	0	1	2	4	6	-2	1

GROUP H

TEAM	PLD	W	D	L	GF	GA	GD	PTS
Belgium	3	3	0	0	4	1	+3	9
Algeria	3	1	1	1	6	5	+1	4
Russia	3	0	2	1	2	3	-1	2
South Korea	3	0	1	2	3	6	-3	1

Second round: Brazil 1-1 Chile (3-2 on pens)
Colombia 2-0 Uruguay • France 2-0 Nigeria
Germany 2-1 Algeria • Netherlands 2-1 Mexico
Costa Rica 1-1 Greece (5-3 on pens)
Argentina 1-0 Switzerland • Belgium 2-1 United States

Quarter-finals: Brazil 2-1 Colombia • France 0-1 Germany
Netherlands 0-0 Costa Rica (4-3 on pens)
Argentina 1-0 Belgium

Semi-finals: Brazil 1-7 Germany
Netherlands 0-0 Argentina (2-4 on pens)

Third place: Brazil 0-3 Netherlands

FINAL

13th July – 16:00
Attendance – 74,738
Estadio do Maracanã (Rio de Janeiro)

GERMANY 1-0 ARGENTINA (AET)

Mario Götze 113'

INDEX

ACKNOWLEDGEMENTS

The following people made this book happen:

My agent Rick Mayston of Agent Fox Media. John Battsek at Passion Pictures enabled the whole project to happen. Dan Gordon from VeryMuchSo with whom I did all the interviews. Steve Macleod at Metro Imaging where all the printing was done. Sean Mulcahy who made the prints. Steve Knight at Direct Photographic who supplied all the kit. Lynda Hall and Mark Graham with whom I made the pilot and the team at ESPN who took it up. And Trevor Davies and Pauline Bache at Octopus Books.

The crew included Jess Ludgrove who produced the whole project, Stevie Haywood, Charlie Grainger, Nick Bennett, Gretha Viana, Maria Asanti, Diego Robino, Erik Winker and Brian Manoukin.

Also Jim Boyce, formerly of FIFA, Pedro Donald, Petra Flueckiger and Dominique Boyer currently at FIFA, Philip Donald, Dean Barrett, Martin Brierley and Valy Domoulin.

And Clare Donald, Becan Donald and Sorcha Donald.

And all the players who scored goals in FIFA World Cup™ Finals

Thank you.

Picture credits

FIFA Spain 122, 128, 134, 213. **Getty Images** 107; Allsport/Hulton Archive 26, 108; Antonio Scorza/AFP 179; Ben Radford 191; Bentley Archive/Popperfoto 61; Bernard Bisson/Sygma via Getty Images 175; Bettmann 58, 62, 122; Bob Thomas 8 left, 9 left, 9 right, 90, 93, 126, 128, 136, 138, 140, 143, 144, 158, 213, 215, 219; Bob Thomas/Popperfoto 13, 205; Bongarts 6; Cattani/Fox Photos 50; Christian Liewig/TempSport/Corbis via Getty Images 172; Damien Meyer/AFP 185; David Cannon 153; Dimitri Iundt/Corbis/VCG via Getty Images 180; Ed Lacey/Popperfoto 209; Evening Standard 46; Gabriel Bouys/AFP 217; Haynes Archive/Popperfoto 206; Horstmüller/ullstein bild via Getty Images 94, 98, 103; Jean-Yves Ruszniewski 160; Jean-Yves Ruszniewski/TempSport/Corbis/VCG via Getty Images 214; Jeff Mitchell - FIFA/FIFA via Getty Images 197; Keystone-France/Gamma-Keystone via Getty Images 43, 208; Laurence Griffiths 220; Manny Millan/Sports Illustrated 104, 110, 114; Mario De Biasi/Mondadori Portfolio via Getty Images 69; Matthew Ashton 198; Metin Pala/Anadolu Agency 201; Neil Leifer/Sports Illustrated 49, 88; Popperfoto 16, 19, 22, 25, 55, 66, 76, 82, 84; Rolls Press/Popperfoto 210; sampics/Corbis via Getty Images 221; Shaun Botterill - FIFA/FIFA via Getty Images 202; STAFF/AFP 154, 157, 212; The Asahi Shimbun via Getty Images 182; Tim de Waele/Corbis via Getty Images 186. **Offside** 8 right, 216, 218; Archivi Farabola 40, 44; Best Photo Agency 10, 14; Gerry Cranham 52, 56; John Varley 120; L'Equipe 20, 28, 32, 34, 37, 38, 65, 132, 194, 207; Witters 100. **Photoshot** Imago 211; Picture Alliance 87, 131, 150, 163, 164; Talking Sport 31, 72, 75. **Press Association Images** Roland Witschel/DPA 125; Werner Baum/DPA 113. **REX Shutterstock** Cesare Galimberti 70; Colorsport 78, 81, 116, 119, 146, 149, 169, 170, 176; Michael Hanschke/Epa 188. **TopFoto** PA Photos 97, 134; ullsteinbild 166.